THE COMPLETE
COOKBOOK

FOR YOUNG SCIENTISTS

AMERICA'S TEST KITCHEN

OTHER COOKBOOKS BY AMERICA'S TEST KITCHEN KIDS

The Complete Cookbook for Young Chefs
#1 *New York Times* best seller, 2019 IACP Cookbook Award winner for Children, Youth & Family

The Complete Baby and Toddler Cookbook
2020 IACP Cookbook Award nominee for Children, Youth & Family

The Complete Baking Book for Young Chefs
New York Times best seller, 2020 IACP Cookbook Award winner for Children, Youth & Family

My First Cookbook

The Complete DIY Cookbook for Young Chefs

PRAISE FOR AMERICA'S TEST KITCHEN KIDS

"The inviting, encouraging tone, which never talks down to the audience; emphasis on introducing and reinforcing basic skills; and approachable, simplified recipes make this a notable standout among cookbooks for kids."
—*Booklist*, starred review, on *The Complete Cookbook for Young Chefs*

"A must-have book . . . a great holiday buy, too." —*School Library Journal*, on *The Complete Cookbook for Young Chefs*

"Inspiring not just a confidence in executing delicious recipes but encouraging them to build foundational kitchen skills." —The Takeout, on *The Complete Cookbook for Young Chefs*

"What a great way to encourage a child to find fun in the kitchen!"
—Tribune Content Agency, on *The Complete Cookbook for Young Chefs*

"The perfect gift . . . Any kid who spends enough time with this book will learn enough to at least make their own school lunches—if not the occasional family meal." —Epicurious, on *The Complete Cookbook for Young Chefs*

"For kids who are interested in cooking . . . [*The Complete Cookbook for Young Chefs*] introduces kids to all the basics . . . and of course there's a whole lot of easy and very tasty recipes to try." —NPR's *Morning Edition*, on *The Complete Cookbook for Young Chefs*

"Having cooked through several cookbooks from America's Test Kitchen, I have come to expect thoroughness, thoughtfulness, attention to detail and helpful troubleshooting, all of which create delicious results. It comes as no surprise that when ATK decided to create a cookbook for kids, *The Complete Cookbook for Young Chefs*, the same standards applied." —*Dallas Morning News*, on *The Complete Cookbook for Young Chefs*

"America's Test Kitchen has long been a reliable source of advice for home cooks. The kitchen tests tools, techniques and recipes before making recommendations through its TV show, magazines and cookbooks. Now, all that know-how is becoming accessible to kids in *The Complete Cookbook for Young Chefs*." —NPR, on *The Complete Cookbook for Young Chefs*

"This book makes baking accessible . . . An inclusive and welcoming text for young chefs." —*Booklist*, on *The Complete Baking Book for Young Chefs*

"A must-have book to keep your young adult cookbook section up-to-date and to support the current trend of creative young bakers. A contemporary and educational cookbook that's once again kid-tested and kid-approved." —*School Library Journal*, starred review, on *The Complete Baking Book for Young Chefs*

"The cooks at America's Test Kitchen have done a wonderful job of assembling appetizing and slyly audacious recipes for babies and young children." —*Wall Street Journal*, on *The Complete Baby and Toddler Cookbook*

"This wonderfully interactive, non-messy introduction to baking, though especially designed for preschoolers, will be an instant hit with readers of all ages." —*School Library Journal*, on *Stir Crack Whisk Bake*

"The story is a fun concept, and Tarkela's realistic digital illustration offers the pleasing details of a television studio." —*Publishers Weekly*, on *Cookies for Santa*

"This is the perfect subscription for the kid who loves food, picky eaters who you want to get into more adventurous foods, parents who want to share cooking fun with their kids, and generally, any kid who is up for a fun activity." —PopSugar, on The Young Chefs' Club

"Kids will love the colorful site and its plentiful selection of recipes, projects, and cooking lessons." —*USA Today*, on America's Test Kitchen Kids website

Library of Congress Cataloging-in-Publication Data

Names: America's Test Kitchen (Firm), author.
Title: The complete cookbook for young scientists : [good science makes great food: 70+ recipes, experiments, & activities] / America's Test Kitchen.
Description: Boston : America's Test Kitchen, [2021] | Includes index. |
  Audience: Ages 8-13 | Audience: Grades 4-6
Identifiers: LCCN 2021014048 (print) | LCCN 2021014049 (ebook) | ISBN
  9781948703666 (hardcover) | ISBN 9781948703673 (ebook)
Subjects: LCSH: Cooking--Juvenile literature. | LCGFT: Cookbooks.
Classification: LCC TX652.5 .A4567 2021 (print) | LCC TX652.5 (ebook) | DDC 641.5/123--dc23
LC record available at https://lccn.loc.gov/2021014048
LC ebook record available at https://lccn.loc.gov/2021014049

AMERICA'S TEST KITCHEN
21 Drydock Avenue, Boston, MA 02210

Printed in Canada
Distributed by Penguin Random House
Publisher Services
Tel: 800.733.3000

FRONT COVER
Photography: Kevin White

Food Styling: Joy Howard

Editor in Chief: Molly Birnbaum

Executive Food Editor: Suzannah McFerran

Executive Editor: Kristin Sargianis

Senior Editors: Ali Velez Alderfer, Afton Cyrus

Test Cooks: Cassandra Loftlin, Andrea Rivera Wawrzyn

Assistant Editors: Tess Berger, Katy O'Hara

Senior Science Research Editor: Paul Adams

Design Director: Lindsey Timko Chandler

Deputy Art Director: Allison Boales

Illustrator: Gabi Homonoff

Photography Director: Julie Bozzo Cote

Photographers: Daniel van Ackere, Steve Klise, Kevin White

Food Styling: Joy Howard, Ashley Moore, Elle Simone Scott, Kendra Smith

Photography Producer: Meredith Mulcahy

Photo Shoot Kitchen Team

   Test Kitchen Director: Erin McMurrer

   Manager: Alli Berkey

   Lead Test Cook: Eric Haessler

Test Cooks: Hannah Fenton, Jacqueline Gochenouer, Gina McCreadie, Christa West

Assistant Test Cooks: Kristen Bango, Hisham Hassan

Senior Manager, Publishing Operations: Taylor Argenzio

Imaging Manager: Lauren Robbins

Production and Imaging Specialists: Dennis Noble, Tricia Neumyer, Amanda Yong

Lead Copy Editor: Rachel Showalter

Copy Editors: Christine Campbell, April Poole

Director of Marketing: Sally Calame

Digital Marketing Manager: Kelsey Hopper

Chief Creative Officer: Jack Bishop

Executive Editorial Directors: Julia Collin Davison, Bridget Lancaster

CONTENTS

INTRODUCTION

Good science makes great food!

At America's Test Kitchen Kids, we get questions about the hows and whys of food and cooking from kids just like you all the time. Why do onions make you cry? Why do some cheeses melt better than others? Can gelatin do anything besides make Jell-O? What *is* gluten, exactly?! These questions are so good that we knew we had to make a book out of them!

In *The Complete Cookbook for Young Scientists* you'll discover the answers to all your questions through superfun science experiments that you can do at home and awesome recipes that you can cook yourself.

This cookbook is kid tested and kid approved. That means that there are thousands of other kids just like you out there making these recipes and experiments and sharing them with their friends and family, loving the process and the results. When making this book, we had more than 12,000 kids testing each and every recipe and experiment, sending us feedback, and letting us know what worked well and what could use improvement. You'll see a handful of these recipe testers in the pages of this book. Thank you to everyone who helped make this book as delicious as possible!

Cooking and baking, whether something new or something familiar, is a science as well as an art. Don't be surprised if you have questions as you begin to operate in the kitchen on your own (never hesitate to ask a grown up!) and if you make some mistakes (we've all been there, many times). Mistakes are an important part of the learning process in the kitchen.

But the most important thing to remember as you begin cooking is to have fun! Use this book to be creative, to try out new things, and to experiment. Be proud of everything you're about to accomplish.

READY, SET, SCIENCE!

UNDERSTANDING THE SYMBOLS IN THIS BOOK

To help you find the right recipe, experiment, or activity for you, this book relies on a system of symbols to quickly show the skill level as well as type of cooking required.

 = **beginner**

 = **intermediate**

 = **advanced**

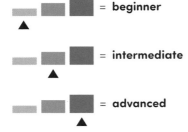 = requires use of **knife**

= requires use of **microwave**

= requires use of **stovetop**

= requires use of **oven**

= **no knives or heat** required

KITCHEN SAFETY TIPS

1. Wash your hands before cooking.

2. Wash your hands after touching raw meat, chicken, fish, or eggs.

3. If you have long hair, tie it back, away from your face.

4. Knives and stoves can be dangerous. Always ask an adult for help if you're in doubt.

5. Hot stovetops and ovens can cause painful burns. Assume that anything on the stovetop (including the pan's handle and lid) is hot. Everything inside the oven is definitely hot. Always use oven mitts.

6. Never let foods you'll eat raw (such as berries) touch foods you'll need to cook (such as raw eggs).

7. Don't ever leave something on the stove unattended. Always turn off the stove and oven when you're done.

HOW TO USE THE RECIPES IN THIS BOOK

Cooking from a recipe is actually a three-step process, and the recipes in this book are written to reflect that, with three distinct sections. The key to successful cooking is, in our humble opinion, all about organization! If you prepare all your ingredients and gather all your equipment before you start cooking, then you won't have to run around the kitchen looking for that last pan or hectically measure out that last cup of flour.

PREPARE INGREDIENTS

Start with the list of ingredients and prepare them as directed. Measure ingredients, melt butter, and chop as needed. Wash fruits and vegetables. You can use small prep bowls to keep ingredients organized.

GATHER COOKING EQUIPMENT

Once all your ingredients are ready, put all the tools you will need to follow the recipe instructions on the counter.

START COOKING!

It's finally time to start cooking. Any ingredients that need to be prepped at the last minute will have instructions within the recipe itself. Don't forget to have fun!

HOW TO USE THE EXPERIMENTS IN THIS BOOK

The goal of an experiment is to answer a question—such as "How do bubbles get into fizzy beverages?"—by gathering data and analyzing it. Just like recipes, experiments follow a step-by-step process, and each step needs to be done in a specific order. And, also just like with cooking, organization is key. If you have all your materials prepared before you start the experiment, you can focus on making important observations.

MATERIALS

Start with the list of materials and prepare them as directed. Most of these materials are food and cooking related, but depending on the experiment, they might include other items from around your house such as markers, masking tape, and even a marble.

MAKE A PREDICTION

Before beginning an experiment, scientists use what they already know to make a prediction—an educated guess—about the answer to the question they're exploring. It helps them (and you!) think through the possibilities and record their ideas.

OBSERVE YOUR RESULTS

Now on to the testing! As you conduct your experiment, carefully observe the results— do your observations support or disprove your prediction? In this book, you'll use all your senses—sight, touch, taste, smell, and hearing— as you make your observations.

UNDERSTANDING YOUR RESULTS

After (and only after!) you've finished your experiment, read an explanation of the science behind your observations and learn more about the results we got when we did the experiment in our Recipe Lab.

EAT YOUR EXPERIMENT

Wherever possible, we encourage you to eat the results of your experiment—this is a cookbook, after all! As you work your way through the experiments in this book, you'll make everything from homemade Greek yogurt to a melted cheese snack to a batch of sugar cookies.

DECODING KITCHENSPEAK

Reading a recipe can sometimes feel like reading a different language. Here are some words that appear in many recipes and what they really mean.

PEEL To remove the outer skin, rind, or layer from food (usually a piece of fruit or a vegetable). Peeling is often done with a vegetable peeler.

ZEST To remove the flavorful, colored skin from a lemon, lime, or orange (the colored skin is called the zest). Zesting does not include removing the bitter white layer (called the pith) under the zest.

CHOP To cut food with a knife into small pieces. Chopped fine = $\frac{1}{8}$- to $\frac{1}{4}$-inch pieces. Chopped = $\frac{1}{4}$- to $\frac{1}{2}$-inch pieces. Chopped coarse = $\frac{1}{2}$- to $\frac{3}{4}$-inch pieces. Use a ruler to understand the different sizes.

SLICE To cut food with a knife into pieces with two flat sides, with the thickness dependent on the recipe instructions. For example, slicing a celery stalk.

GRATE To cut food (often cheese) into very small, uniform pieces using a rasp grater or the small holes of a box grater.

STIR To combine ingredients in a bowl or cooking vessel, often with a rubber spatula or wooden spoon.

TOSS To gently combine ingredients with tongs or two forks and/or spoons in order to distribute the ingredients evenly. You toss salad in a bowl (you don't stir it).

MELT To heat solid food (such as butter) on the stovetop or in the microwave until it becomes a liquid.

SIMMER To heat liquid until small bubbles break often across its surface, as when cooking a soup or sauce.

BOIL To heat liquid until large bubbles break across the surface at a rapid and constant rate, as when cooking pasta.

DECODING EXPERIMENTSPEAK

Reading a science experiment can sometimes feel like reading a different language, too! Here are some common words in many experiments and what they mean.

PREDICTION An educated guess, based on your knowledge and experience, about what will happen in an experiment.

OBSERVATION The act of careful watching, listening, touching, tasting, or smelling. When conducting experiments, scientists record their observations.

VARIABLE Something that can be changed. In experiments, scientists change at least one variable to observe what happens. For example, scientists studying whether the type of sugar affects the flavor and texture of cookies might add brown sugar to one batch of cookies and white sugar to a second batch of cookies. The type of sugar is the variable.

CONTROL A variable that is not changed in an experiment. For example, scientists studying whether the type of sugar affects the flavor and texture of cookies would make sure to use the same cookie ingredients (except the sugar) and bake the cookies at the same temperature for the same amount of time. Those are control variables.

SUBJECT When scientists conduct experiments, their "subjects" are the people whose reactions or responses they're studying.

RESULTS What happens in an experiment—a combination of the observations and measurements recorded and interpreted by scientists.

BLIND When the subjects of an experiment do not know what is being tested. For example, subjects might taste two batches of pasta, one cooked with salt and one cooked without salt, without being told what is different about them.

MOLECULE Something made up of one or more atoms, like the oxygen molecule, which is made of two oxygen atoms.

COMPOUND A type of molecule that's made up of atoms from two or more different elements. Water is made up of the elements hydrogen and oxygen, so we can call it a compound.

PROPERTY A quality, characteristic, or trait of a thing or person. For example, the texture or flavor of a food or ingredient.

FLAVOR A combination of a food's tastes and smells. For example, a food's flavor might be bright, nutty, or tangy.

TEXTURE What food feels like in your hand or in your mouth. For example, a food's texture might be crunchy, smooth, or chewy.

DIFFUSION ("di-FEW-shun") The movement of molecules and ions from places where there are lots of them to places where there are fewer of them.

OSMOSIS ("oz-MOE-sis") The movement of water molecules across a barrier, such as a cell membrane, that lets some (but not all) kinds of molecules through.

HOW TO MEASURE AND WEIGH

For consistent cooking results, it's important to measure accurately. There are two ways to measure ingredients: by weight, using a scale, and by volume, using measuring cups and spoons. Using a scale to weigh your ingredients is the most accurate method. But if you do not have a scale, that's OK! Below are tips on using a scale and how best to measure ingredients if you do not have a scale.

USING A SCALE

Turn on the scale and place the bowl on the scale. Then press the "tare" button to zero out the weight (that means that the weight of the bowl won't be included!).

Slowly add your ingredient to the bowl until you reach the desired weight. Here we are weighing 5 ounces of all-purpose flour (which is equal to 1 cup).

HOW TO MEASURE DRY AND LIQUID INGREDIENTS

Dry ingredients and liquid ingredients are measured differently. Note that small amounts of both dry and liquid ingredients are measured with small measuring spoons.

Dry ingredients should be measured in dry measuring cups—small metal or plastic cups with handles. Each set has cups of varying sizes. Dip the measuring cup into the ingredient and sweep away the excess with the back of a butter knife.

Liquid ingredients (such as milk, water, or juice) should be measured in a liquid measuring cup (a larger, clear plastic or glass cup with lines on the side, a big handle, and a pour spout). Place the measuring cup on the counter and bend down to read the bottom of the concave arc at the liquid's surface. This is known as the meniscus line.

KITCHEN MATH

3 teaspoons = 1 tablespoon
16 tablespoons = 1 cup
16 ounces = 1 pound

2 cups = 1 pint
4 cups = 1 quart
4 quarts = 1 gallon

ESSENTIAL PREP STEPS

HOW TO MELT BUTTER

Butter can be melted in a small saucepan on the stove (use medium-low heat), but we think that using the microwave is easier.

1 Cut butter into 1-tablespoon pieces. Place butter in microwave-safe bowl. Cover bowl with small plate.

2 Place in microwave. Heat butter at 50 percent power until melted, 30 to 60 seconds (longer if melting a lot of butter). Watch butter and stop microwave as soon as butter has melted. Use oven mitts to remove bowl from microwave.

HOW TO SOFTEN BUTTER

When taken straight from the refrigerator, butter is quite firm. For some baking recipes, you need to soften butter before trying to combine it with other ingredients. This is just a fancy term for letting the temperature of butter rise from 35 degrees (its refrigerator temperature) to 65 degrees (cool room temperature). This takes about 1 hour, but here are two ways to speed things up.

Counter Method Cut butter into 1-inch pieces (to create more surface area). Place butter on plate and wait about 30 minutes. Once butter gives to light pressure (try to push your fingertip into butter), it's ready to use.

Microwave Method Cut butter into 1-inch pieces and place on microwave-safe plate. Heat in microwave at 50 percent power for 10 seconds. Check butter with fingertip test. Heat for another 5 to 10 seconds if necessary.

HOW TO CRACK AND SEPARATE EGGS

Unless you are hard-cooking eggs, you need to start by cracking them open. In some recipes, you will need to separate the yolk (the yellow part) and the white (the clear part) and use them differently. Cold eggs are much easier to separate.

1 To crack Gently hit side of egg against flat surface of counter or cutting board.

2 Pull shell apart into 2 pieces over bowl. Let yolk and white drop into bowl. Discard shell.

3 To separate yolk and white Use your hand to very gently transfer yolk to second bowl.

HOW TO GRATE OR SHRED CHEESE

Cheese is often cut into very small pieces to flavor pizza, bread, rolls, and more. When grating or shredding, use a big piece of cheese so that your hand stays safely away from the sharp holes.

1 To grate Hard cheeses such as Parmesan can be rubbed against a rasp grater or the small holes of a box grater to make a fluffy pile of cheese.

2 To shred Semisoft cheeses such as cheddar or mozzarella can be rubbed against the large holes of a box grater to make long pieces of cheese.

HOW TO CHOP OR MINCE FRESH HERBS

Fresh herbs need to be washed and dried before they are chopped (or minced).

1 Use your fingers to remove leaves from stems; discard stems.

2 Gather leaves into small pile. Place 1 hand on handle of chef's knife and rest fingers of your other hand on top of blade. Use rocking motion, pivoting knife as you chop.

HOW TO ZEST AND JUICE CITRUS

The flavorful colored skin from lemons, limes, and oranges (called the zest) is often removed and used in recipes. If you need zest, it's best to zest your fruit before juicing. After juicing, use a small spoon to remove any seeds from the bowl of juice.

1 To zest Rub fruit against rasp grater to remove colored zest. Turn fruit as you go to avoid bitter white layer underneath zest.

2 To juice Cut fruit in half through equator (not through ends).

3 Place 1 half of fruit in citrus juicer. Hold juicer over bowl and squeeze to extract juice.

HOW TO PEEL AND MINCE GARLIC

Garlic is sticky, so you may need to carefully wipe the pieces of garlic from the sides of the knife to get them back onto the cutting board, where you can cut them. You can also use a garlic press to both crush and mince garlic.

1 Crush clove with bottom of measuring cup to loosen papery skin. Use your fingers to remove and discard papery skin.

2 Place 1 hand on handle of chef's knife and rest fingers of your other hand on top of blade. Use rocking motion, pivoting knife as you chop garlic repeatedly to cut it into very small pieces.

HOW TO CHOP ONIONS OR SHALLOTS

Shallots are smaller, milder cousins of onions. If you're working with a small shallot, there's no need to cut it in half.

1 Halve onion through root end, then use your fingers to remove peel. Trim top of onion.

2 Place onion half flat side down. Starting 1 inch from root end, make several vertical cuts.

3 Rotate onion and slice across first cuts. As you slice, onion will fall apart into chopped pieces.

HOW TO PREP CHILES

Chiles contain a compound called capsaicin that makes them spicy. To make sure that you do not get it on your skin or in your eyes, wear disposable gloves when touching chiles.

1 Hold chile firmly with 1 hand, with stem facing out. Use chef's knife to slice off stem and top of chile.

2 Cut chile in half lengthwise (the long way). Use tip of teaspoon to scoop out seeds and ribs from each half. Discard seeds, ribs, and stem.

3 Press 1 half of chile so it lays flat on cutting board, skin side down. Slice chile lengthwise (the long way) into ¼-inch-wide strips. Repeat with remaining chile half.

4 Turn half of strips and cut crosswise (the short way) into ¼-inch pieces. Repeat with remaining half of strips.

HOW TO TELL WHEN MEAT OR FISH IS DONE

One great way to know when thick cuts of chicken, meat, or fish are cooked is to use an instant-read thermometer. To check the temperature, insert the tip of the thermometer into the center of the thickest part of the food, making sure to avoid any bones.

Insert tip of thermometer into thickest part of food. You can use tongs to lift individual pieces of chicken, meat, or fish and then insert thermometer sideways into center of food.

BREAKFAST

WHAT IS GLUTEN ANYWAY?

Gluten is a network of proteins found in many baked goods. Wheat flour contains two kinds of protein, called glutenin ("GLUE-teh-nin") and gliadin ("GLY-a-din"). They are both coiled up pretty tightly—and in dry flour, they stay apart from each other. But when flour is mixed with water, these proteins unfurl and begin to link up. With time, kneading, or mixing, those linked proteins, now called gluten, form a network, kind of like a spiderweb. That network gets stronger with more time, kneading, or mixing, giving baked goods structure and support.

Soft, crumbly, or flaky baked goods such as muffins or Crepes (page 24) don't need a lot of gluten—so we mix batter until it's only "just combined." Breads, on the other hand, often need a lot of gluten. We knead our Cinnamon Swirl Bread (page 26) for 8 minutes!

TAKING DOUGH DOWN
THE HOME STRETCH

What is gluten, and how does it work? Find out in this flour-powered activity. You'll make one dough with a lot of gluten and one dough with none and then STREEEEEETCH them out.

LET'S GO!

1 Use masking tape and marker to label 1 small bowl "Wheat Flour" and second small bowl "Rice Flour."

2 In bowl labeled "Wheat Flour," use spoon to stir and press together all-purpose flour and 5 teaspoons water until shaggy dough forms, about 1 minute.

3 Sprinkle counter with extra all-purpose flour. Transfer dough to counter. Use your hands to gather dough into loose ball and knead dough (see page 28) until smooth, 3 to 4 minutes. Shape dough into ball and wrap with plastic wrap. Return wrapped dough to bowl labeled "Wheat Flour."

4 Repeat steps 2 and 3 with rice flour and water in bowl labeled "Rice Flour." Let both doughs rest for 10 minutes.

5 **MAKE A PREDICTION** Do you think the wheat flour dough and the rice flour dough will behave the same or differently when you try to pull them apart? Why?

TOTAL TIME: 40 minutes

LEVEL:

MATERIALS

Masking tape

Marker

2 small bowls

2 spoons

¼ cup (1¼ ounces) all-purpose flour, plus extra for counter

1-teaspoon measuring spoon

Water

Plastic wrap

¼ cup (1¼ ounces) white rice flour, plus extra for counter

KEEP GOING!

TESTING THE DOUGH

After 10 minutes, unwrap ball of wheat flour dough. Use your hands to gently pull the dough apart until it breaks. Repeat with rice flour dough.

6 After 10 minutes, unwrap ball of wheat flour dough. Use your hands to gently pull dough apart until it breaks (see photo, left). Repeat with rice flour dough.

7 **OBSERVE YOUR RESULTS** What happened to each type of dough as you pulled it apart? Did they behave the same or differently? How so? Which dough could you stretch farther?

STOP UNDERSTANDING YOUR RESULTS

(Don't read until you've completed the experiment!)

THE BIG IDEAS

- Gluten is a strong, stretchy web of proteins that forms when wheat flour is mixed with water and then stirred or kneaded.
- A strong gluten network gives many baked goods, such as breads, their tall height and chewy texture.
- Soft, tender baked goods, such as cakes, have only a little bit of gluten.

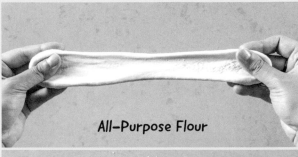

All-Purpose Flour

Rice Flour

In our Recipe Lab, we found that stretching the dough made from all-purpose (wheat) flour was very different from stretching the dough made from rice flour. The wheat dough stretched nearly 8 inches before breaking, while the rice dough didn't stretch at all. Gluten is what makes wheat doughs stretchy and elastic and gives baked goods much of their texture and their shape.

Where does gluten come from?

Gluten starts to form when wheat flour and water mix. Proteins in the flour link up and form long, stretchy chains of gluten. Stirring and kneading helps the gluten become a strong network. The more you stir a batter or knead a dough, the stronger the gluten network becomes. After kneading, you often let dough rest for a while. This lets the gluten network relax, so it's easier to stretch.

Why is gluten so important?

A strong, stretchy gluten network is what lets dough rise. As leaveners create gas bubbles in the dough, gluten traps the gas inside— like lots of tiny balloons in the dough. The pockets of trapped gas become the air bubbles inside the finished product. Without

gluten, that gas would escape and the bread wouldn't rise.

But what if you want to make something soft and tender, such as a cake, cookies, or Crepes (page 24)? Then you want only a little bit of gluten to form. Stirring the ingredients just enough to combine them creates a small amount of gluten. That means your finished product will be soft and easy to bite into.

What about gluten-free flour?

Rice flour, made from ground-up rice, doesn't create gluten when it's mixed with water. The proteins in rice flour are different than those in wheat flour, so they make a different, nonstretchy dough. Rice flour is typically used to make things like rice noodles and a sweet Japanese dessert called mochi. It's also in many gluten-free flour blends.

recipe

CREPES

Just a little bit of gluten keeps these fancy French pancakes tender and soft.

SERVES: 4 (Makes 10 crepes)

TOTAL TIME: 45 minutes

LEVEL: ▲

PREPARE INGREDIENTS

- ½ teaspoon vegetable oil
- 1 cup (5 ounces) all-purpose flour
- 1 teaspoon sugar
- ¼ teaspoon salt
- 1½ cups (12 ounces) whole milk
- 3 large eggs
- 2 tablespoons unsalted butter, melted and cooled (see page 13)

FILLING AND TOPPING IDEAS

Sweet: Nutella, jam, sliced bananas, sliced strawberries, or sugar; dust with confectioners' (powdered) sugar

Savory: Shredded or crumbled cheese, ham, or scrambled eggs; chopped herbs or sliced scallions

GATHER COOKING EQUIPMENT

- 10-inch nonstick skillet
- Paper towels
- 2 bowls (1 large, 1 medium)
- Whisk
- Cooling rack
- ¼-cup dry measuring cup
- Spatula
- 2 large microwave-safe plates
- Oven mitts

START COOKING!

1. Add oil to 10-inch nonstick skillet. Use paper towel to spread oil into thin, even coating on bottom of skillet. Discard paper towel. Heat skillet over low heat for at least 5 minutes.

2. While skillet is heating, in large bowl, whisk together flour, sugar, and salt. In medium bowl, whisk together milk and eggs.

3. Add half of milk mixture to flour mixture and whisk until smooth. Add melted butter and whisk until combined. Add remaining milk mixture and whisk until smooth.

4. Set cooling rack next to stove. Increase heat to medium and heat skillet for 1 more minute.

5. Use ¼-cup dry measuring cup to portion first crepe following photos, right.

6. Return skillet to heat and cook until surface looks dry and crepe starts to brown at edges, 1 to 1½ minutes. Working quickly, slide spatula under crepe and flip crepe. Cook until second side is spotty brown, 15 to 30 seconds.

7. Carefully slide crepe from skillet onto cooling rack (use spatula to help transfer if needed). Return skillet to heat. Repeat steps 5 and 6 with remaining batter, stacking cooked crepes on top of each other on cooling rack. Turn off heat.

8. Transfer stack of crepes to large microwave-safe plate. Place second plate, upside down, on top of crepes. Heat in microwave until warm, 30 to 60 seconds. Use oven mitts to remove from microwave and remove top plate. Fill crepes with your favorite fillings, fold in half or into quarters, and top with your favorite toppings. Serve.

MAKING CREPES

1 Use ¼-cup dry measuring cup to scoop ¼ cup batter from bowl. Lift skillet off heat and pour batter into far side of skillet.

2 Swirl skillet gently in circles and shake until batter evenly covers bottom of skillet.

Tender French Pancakes

Crepes are thin, tender, delicate pancakes that are a popular street food in France. The key to tender crepes is forming just a little gluten in the batter. To do this, our crepe batter contains a lot more liquid (1½ cups of milk and three eggs) than flour (just 1 cup). All that liquid makes it harder for the proteins in the flour to find each other, link up, and form a network of gluten. Since just a small amount of gluten forms in the batter, our crepes' texture stays extra-soft and tender.

CINNAMON SWIRL BREAD

What gives this loaf of bread its height and texture—and keeps that signature swirl in place? Gluten, and lots of it!

SERVES: 10 (Makes 1 loaf)

TOTAL TIME: 2 hours, plus 1½ hours rising time, plus 2 hours cooling time

LEVEL:

PREPARE INGREDIENTS

- 1 cup (8 ounces) milk
- 3 tablespoons plus 1 tablespoon unsalted butter, measured separately
- ½ cup (3½ ounces) sugar
- 3 tablespoons packed brown sugar
- 2 teaspoons ground cinnamon
- 3 cups (15 ounces) all-purpose flour
- 1½ teaspoons instant or rapid-rise yeast
- 1 teaspoon salt
- 2 large egg yolks (see page 14)
- Vegetable oil spray
- 1 teaspoon water

GATHER COOKING EQUIPMENT

- 4-cup liquid measuring cup
- Rubber spatula
- 3 bowls (1 large, 1 medium, 1 small microwave-safe)
- Whisk
- 1-tablespoon measuring spoon
- Stand mixer with dough hook attachment
- Plastic wrap
- 8½-by-4½-inch metal loaf pan
- Ruler
- Pastry brush
- ½-cup dry measuring cup
- Oven mitts
- Cooling rack
- Butter knife
- Cutting board
- Bread knife

START COOKING!

1. Place milk and 3 tablespoons butter in 4-cup liquid measuring cup. Heat in microwave for 1 minute. Stir mixture with rubber spatula. Continue to heat in microwave until butter is melted, about 1 minute. Remove from microwave and let milk mixture cool until just warm, about 20 minutes.

2. While milk mixture cools, in medium bowl, whisk together sugar, brown sugar, and cinnamon. Measure 3 tablespoons cinnamon sugar into bowl of stand mixer. Set aside remaining cinnamon sugar mixture to use in steps 8 and 11.

3. Add flour, yeast, and salt to stand mixer bowl with cinnamon sugar and whisk until combined. Lock bowl into place and attach dough hook to stand mixer.

4. When milk mixture is just warm, add egg yolks to liquid measuring cup and whisk until combined.

KEEP GOING! ↻

The Need to Knead

This loaf of bread needs to be tall and sturdy in order to support all that cinnamon swirl filling. To get that sturdiness, you need to knead! Kneading is the process of pushing and pulling dough over and over. It's an important part of bread making because kneading helps the proteins in the flour link together and create a strong, stretchy network of gluten. The longer you knead the dough, the stronger that gluten network will be, making your bread sturdier and chewier. You can knead bread dough by hand, but it would take about 25 minutes of kneading to develop enough gluten for this bread. To save time (and our arms), we use a stand mixer in this recipe. The mixer's powerful motor spins the dough hook, which pushes the dough against the side of the mixer bowl to knead it, developing all the gluten we need in just 8 minutes.

5. Start mixer on low speed and slowly pour in milk mixture. Mix until no dry flour is visible, about 2 minutes. Increase speed to medium and knead dough for 8 minutes. Stop mixer.

6. Transfer dough to clean counter and knead dough for 30 seconds, then form dough into smooth ball.

7. Spray large bowl with vegetable oil spray. Place dough in greased bowl and cover with plastic wrap. Let dough rise until doubled in size, 1 to 1½ hours.

8. Spray inside bottom and sides of 8½-by-4½-inch metal loaf pan with vegetable oil spray. Transfer dough to clean counter and shape, fill, and roll up dough following photos, page 29.

9. Spray sheet of plastic with vegetable oil spray. Cover loaf pan loosely with greased plastic and let dough rise at room temperature until dough is level with top edge of pan, 30 to 45 minutes.

10. While dough rises, adjust oven rack to middle position and heat oven to 350 degrees.

11. When dough is ready, melt remaining 1 tablespoon butter in small microwave-safe bowl (see page 13). Discard plastic from loaf pan. Use pastry brush to gently brush top of loaf with melted butter. Sprinkle evenly with remaining cinnamon sugar.

12. Place loaf pan in oven. Bake until top is deep brown, 45 to 55 minutes. Use oven mitts to remove pan from oven and place on cooling rack (ask an adult for help). Let bread cool in pan for 15 minutes.

13. Carefully run butter knife around edges of bread to loosen from loaf pan (ask an adult for help—pan will be hot). Use oven mitts to carefully turn pan on its side and remove bread from pan. Let bread cool completely on cooling rack, about 2 hours. Transfer bread to cutting board, slice (ask an adult for help), and serve. (Bread can be stored in airtight container at room temperature for up to 3 days.)

1 Transfer dough to clean counter and use your hands to gently press down on dough to pop any large bubbles. Pat dough into 18-by-7-inch rectangle with short edge facing you.

2 Use pastry brush to lightly paint dough with water.

3 Use ½-cup dry measuring cup to measure ½ cup reserved cinnamon sugar from bowl and sprinkle over dough, leaving 2-inch border along top.

4 Use bottom of measuring cup to gently press cinnamon sugar into dough. (Save remaining cinnamon sugar in bowl for sprinkling over top in step 11.)

5 Starting at short edge closest to you, roll up dough into log.

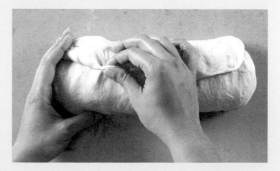

6 Use your fingers to pinch seam and ends closed. Place loaf seam side down in greased loaf pan.

WHAT'S THE DIFFERENCE BETWEEN egg whites AND egg yolks?

An egg is really two ingredients—an egg yolk and an egg white—in a single package, the shell. Egg whites and yolks contain different amounts of water, protein, and fat. That means that they react very differently to cooking, especially temperature (learn more in the experiment on page 31).

You can cook eggs so many different ways—fried, hard-cooked, soft-cooked, poached, scrambled, and more. We chose two VERY different recipes to demonstrate the eggy possibilities. For Huevos Rancheros (page 34), which means "ranch-style eggs" in Spanish, we cook the eggs right in their sauce. For Cloud Eggs (page 36) we whip the whites into a fluffy cloud and bake the yolks nestled within it.

A SCIENCE EGGSPERIMENT

In this experiment, you'll discover how egg yolks and egg whites cook differently and learn what they're made of. You'll also make some cooked eggs—you can eat them for breakfast!

TOTAL TIME: 45 minutes

LEVEL:

MATERIALS

Masking tape

Permanent marker

Serving platter

3 large eggs, cold

Medium saucepan with lid

Water

Steamer basket

Oven mitts

3 cups ice

Liquid measuring cup

Medium bowl

Slotted spoon

Butter knife

LET'S GO!

1 Make 3 masking tape labels. Use permanent marker to write "7 minutes" on 1 label, "10 minutes" on second label, and "13 minutes" on third label. Place labels around edge of serving platter. Set aside platter.

2 Use permanent marker to write "7" on 1 egg's shell, "10" on second egg's shell, and "13" on third egg's shell.

3 Fill medium saucepan with about 1 inch water. Bring water to rolling boil (lots of big bubbles will break surface of water) over high heat.

4 Place eggs in steamer basket. Use oven mitts to carefully lower basket into saucepan (see photo, page 32) (ask an adult for help). Eggs can be above or partly under water.

5 Cover saucepan and reduce heat to medium-low. While eggs cook, combine ice and 3 cups cold water in medium bowl.

KEEP GOING! ↷

STEAMING EGGS

1 Place eggs in steamer basket. Use oven mitts to carefully lower basket into saucepan (ask an adult for help). Eggs can be above or partly under water.

2 After specified time for each egg, transfer each egg to ice bath. Make sure to replace lid on saucepan after you transfer each egg. Let eggs sit in ice bath for 5 minutes.

Eat Your Experiment!

You can eat your eggs plain, sprinkle them with **salt** or a dash of **hot sauce**, or serve them with a side of **toast**.

6 MAKE A PREDICTION What do you think the egg whites and egg yolks will look like after they have cooked for 7 minutes, 10 minutes, and 13 minutes?

7 After 7 minutes, use slotted spoon to transfer egg labeled "7" to ice bath (see photo, left). Cover saucepan. After 10 minutes, use slotted spoon to transfer egg labeled "10" to ice bath. Cover saucepan. After 13 minutes, use slotted spoon to transfer egg labeled "13" to ice bath. Turn off heat. Let eggs sit in ice bath for 5 minutes.

8 After 5 minutes, remove eggs from ice bath. Starting with egg labeled "7," crack egg against hard surface (such as a counter) and peel away shell with your hands. Discard shell. Place egg in front of "7 minutes" label on serving platter. Use butter knife to slice egg in half lengthwise (the long way). Repeat with eggs labeled "10" and "13."

9 OBSERVE YOUR RESULTS Do the egg yolks and egg whites look the same or different in each egg? How does a longer cooking time change the egg yolk and egg white?

STOP UNDERSTANDING YOUR RESULTS
(Don't read until you've completed the experiment!)

Here's what our eggs looked like after cooking for 7 minutes, 10 minutes, and 13 minutes. Did your eggs look similar?

7-Minute Egg
Solid white
Runny, liquid yolk

10-Minute Egg
Solid white
Gooey, mostly solid yolk

13-Minute Egg
Solid white
Completely solid yolk

THE BIG IDEAS

- Egg whites and egg yolks are made of different materials, and they cook (turn from a solid to a liquid) at different temperatures.
- Whole eggs cook from the outside in—the egg white, closest to the shell, heats up and starts cooking first.

To understand why the egg whites were fully cooked before the egg yolks became solid, we need to crack the eggstraordinary science of eggs.

When you cook eggs, both the yolk and the white start out as liquids and become solid when they reach a certain temperature (more on that in a minute).

Egg whites are made of mostly water and some protein, while egg yolks are made of a combination of water, fat, and protein. Because they're made up of different things, egg whites and egg yolks react differently to heat.

Egg whites start to change from liquid to solid when they reach about 145 degrees and are completely solid and ready to eat when they reach 180 degrees. Egg yolks, on the other hand, start to become solid at 150 degrees and are completely solid at 158 degrees.

Why are these temperatures so important? Well, if you're trying to cook an egg so that the white is solid and the yolk is still runny and liquid, you need to cook the egg white to a much higher temperature (180 degrees) than you do the egg yolk. (Remember: Egg yolks become solid at 158 degrees.) And if your goal is a fully solid egg yolk, you don't want it to get much hotter than 158 degrees or your yolk will have a dry, chalky texture.

One thing is working in your favor, though: Egg whites cook faster than egg yolks because they're on the outside, closer to the shell and closer to the heat source. As the egg cooks inside the steamy saucepan, heat moves through the shell, into the white, and, finally, into the yolk.

HUEVOS RANCHEROS

SERVES: 4

TOTAL TIME: 1 hour

LEVEL:

In this recipe, the huevos ("eggs" in Spanish) cook right in the simmering sauce. Chiles contain a compound called capsaicin that makes them spicy. To make sure you do not get it in your eyes, wear disposable gloves when touching chiles.

PREPARE INGREDIENTS

- 1 (28-ounce) can diced tomatoes, opened
- 2 tablespoons vegetable oil
- 1 small onion, peeled and chopped (see page 16)
- 1–2 jalapeño chiles, stemmed, halved, and seeded, cut into 1-inch pieces (see page 17)
- 2 tablespoons chili powder
- 1 tablespoon tomato paste
- 2 garlic cloves, lightly crushed and peeled (see page 16)
- 1½ teaspoons packed brown sugar
- 1 teaspoon salt
- 1 tablespoon lime juice, squeezed from ½ lime (see page 15)
- 1 cup shredded Monterey Jack cheese (4 ounces)
- 4 large eggs
- 2 tablespoons minced fresh cilantro (see page 15)
- 4 (6-inch) corn tortillas

GATHER COOKING EQUIPMENT

Fine-mesh strainer	Ruler
Large bowl	Small bowl
Rubber spatula	Oven mitts
12-inch nonstick skillet with lid	Small microwave-safe plate
Food processor	Dish towel

START COOKING!

1. Set fine-mesh strainer over large bowl. Pour tomatoes into fine-mesh strainer. Use rubber spatula to stir and press on tomatoes to remove liquid.

2. Heat oil in 12-inch nonstick skillet over medium heat for 1 minute (oil should be hot but not smoking). Add onion and jalapeños and cook, stirring often with rubber spatula, until well browned, about 8 minutes.

3. Add chili powder, tomato paste, garlic, brown sugar, and salt to skillet and stir to combine. Cook for 30 seconds. Turn off heat and slide skillet to cool burner.

4. Carefully transfer onion mixture to food processor (ask an adult for help). Add drained tomatoes and lime juice and lock lid into place. Hold down pulse button for 1 second, then release. Repeat until tomatoes are coarsely chopped, about ten 1-second pulses.

5. Remove lid and carefully remove processor blade (ask an adult for help). Use rubber spatula to transfer tomato mixture to now-empty skillet.

6. Spread tomato mixture into even layer in skillet. Sprinkle Monterey Jack evenly over top. Make shallow holes in sauce and fill with eggs following photos, right.

7. Bring tomato mixture to simmer (small bubbles should break often across surface of mixture) over medium heat. Reduce heat to medium-low. Cover skillet and cook, 5 to 6 minutes for slightly runny yolks (white around edge of yolk will be barely opaque) or 7 to 8 minutes for soft but set yolks.

8. Turn off heat and slide skillet to cool burner. Use oven mitts to remove lid. Sprinkle with cilantro. Stack tortillas on microwave-safe plate and cover with damp dish towel. Heat in microwave until warm, about 1 minute. Serve immediately with warm tortillas.

MAKING HUEVOS RANCHEROS

1 Use rubber spatula to make 4 shallow holes (about 3 inches wide) in tomato mixture.

2 Crack 1 egg into small bowl. Carefully pour egg into first hole. Repeat with remaining 3 eggs, cracking and pouring 1 egg into each hole.

Even Steamin'

Cooking eggs directly in the sauce and covering the skillet helps our huevos cook evenly. The bottom and sides of each egg are in contact with the hot sauce, and the trapped steam helps cook the tops!

recipe

CLOUD EGGS

Whip up protein-heavy egg whites to create a light, cloudlike breakfast. Cloud eggs are a tasty (and beautiful) breakfast on their own, or you can serve them on top of a piece of toast.

SERVES: 4

TOTAL TIME: 40 minutes

LEVEL:

PREPARE INGREDIENTS

Vegetable oil spray

4 large eggs

¼ teaspoon cream of tartar

Pinch salt

GATHER COOKING EQUIPMENT

Rimmed baking sheet

Parchment paper

5 small bowls (If you're short on small bowls, you can use small ramekins, mugs, or teacups)

Electric mixer (stand mixer with whisk attachment or handheld mixer and large bowl)

Rubber spatula

Spoon

Aluminum foil

Oven mitts

Cooling rack

Spatula

4 serving plates

START COOKING!

1. Adjust oven rack to middle position and heat oven to 350 degrees. Line rimmed baking sheet with parchment paper and spray with vegetable oil spray.

2. Spray 4 small bowls with vegetable oil spray. Separate egg whites from egg yolks (following photos, page 14), placing each yolk in separate greased small bowl and placing all whites in bowl of stand mixer (or large bowl if using handheld mixer).

3. Add cream of tartar and salt to egg whites. If using stand mixer, lock bowl into place and attach whisk attachment to stand mixer. Start mixer on medium-low speed and whip mixture until foamy, about 1 minute. Increase speed to medium-high and whip until stiff peaks form, 3 to 4 minutes.

4. Shape 4 cloud eggs following photos, right. Spray aluminum foil with vegetable oil spray and place over baking sheet—do NOT crimp edges or cover tightly.

5. Place baking sheet in oven and bake until whites are firm and yolks are cooked to your preference: 12 to 14 minutes for slightly runny yolks, 15 to 17 minutes for soft but set yolks, or 18 to 20 minutes for set and firm yolks. (To check if your Cloud Eggs are done, use oven mitts to carefully lift foil and peek at eggs—ask an adult for help.)

6. Use oven mitts to remove baking sheet from oven (ask an adult for help). Place baking sheet on cooling rack. Use spatula to transfer eggs to serving plates. Serve.

HOW TO SHAPE CLOUD EGGS

1 Use rubber spatula to spoon whipped egg white mixture onto parchment-lined baking sheet in 4 even mounds. Use back of spoon to make small well in each mound.

2 Carefully slide 1 egg yolk into well of each egg white mound.

"Eggsquisite" Egg Science

Egg whites are made of mostly water and protein. Whipping egg whites causes their naturally tangled proteins to unfold and form a kind of net that traps air inside. The proteins reinforce the bubble walls in the egg white foam, making it strong. Cream of tartar helps reinforce the proteins. In the hot oven, water evaporates, leaving a cloudlike solid after baking.

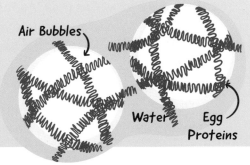

Air Bubbles

Water   Egg Proteins

WHAT CAN YOU DO WITH *yogurt*?

Humans have been making yogurt for thousands of years. Around the world you'll find lots of different styles. Different varieties include thick and creamy Greek yogurt (see page 41), tart and tangy skyr ("skeer") or Icelandic yogurt, smooth and creamy Australian yogurt, and thin and loose Bulgarian yogurt. Yogurt can be made from many types of milk—from cow or sheep to coconut or soy milk. All yogurt is made by adding live (friendly!) bacteria to warm milk. As they hang out in the milk, the bacteria produce something called lactic acid. Lactic acid helps thicken the milk and gives yogurt its signature tangy flavor.

There are so many different ways to eat yogurt. Go for it plain; use it to make colorful Pineapple-Mango Smoothie Bowls (page 42); or use it in baked goods like Mixed Berry Muffins (page 44).

activity

IT'S . . . GREEK TO ME

In this activity, you'll discover the difference between regular yogurt and Greek yogurt—and make a creamy, delicious breakfast, too! Do not use yogurt containing modified food starch, gelatin, pectin, or ingredients called "gums." You can use three basket-style paper coffee filters instead of the cheesecloth.

TOTAL TIME: 15 minutes, plus 8 hours straining time

LEVEL: ▬ ▬ ▬
         ▲

LET'S GO!

1 Line fine-mesh strainer with double layer of cheesecloth. Set strainer over large bowl. (There should be at least 2 inches between bottom of bowl and bottom of strainer.)

2 Use spoon to scoop spoonful of yogurt into small bowl. Taste yogurt: How would you describe the flavor? What is the texture like? Is it thin? Thick? Creamy?

3 Use large spoon to transfer remaining yogurt to cheesecloth-lined strainer (see photo, page 40). Cover strainer and bowl tightly with plastic wrap. Place in refrigerator and chill for at least 8 hours or up to 24 hours.

4 **MAKE A PREDICTION** What do you think will happen to the yogurt as it sits in the strainer? Will its flavor change? Its texture?

MATERIALS

Fine-mesh strainer

Cheesecloth

3 bowls (1 large, 2 small)

Spoon

2 cups plain whole-milk yogurt

Large spoon

Plastic wrap

Liquid measuring cup

Airtight container

KEEP GOING! ↱

STRAINING YOGURT

Use large spoon to transfer remaining yogurt to cheesecloth-lined strainer. Cover strainer and bowl tightly with plastic wrap. Place in refrigerator and chill for at least 8 hours or up to 24 hours.

Eat Your Activity!

Yogurt can be stored in refrigerator for up to 1 week. Serve plain or top with **honey**, **fruit**, and **granola**.

5 **OBSERVE YOUR RESULTS** Remove bowl and strainer from refrigerator. Set aside strainer. Pour liquid from bowl into liquid measuring cup. Record how much liquid drained from yogurt. Discard liquid.

6 Use clean large spoon to transfer yogurt from strainer into empty liquid measuring cup and record amount of yogurt. Discard cheesecloth.

7 Transfer yogurt to airtight container. Use clean spoon to scoop spoonful of yogurt into second small bowl. Taste yogurt: How would you describe its flavor? Its texture? Has the yogurt changed after sitting in the cheesecloth?

STOP UNDERSTANDING YOUR RESULTS
(Don't read until you've completed the activity!)

THE BIG IDEAS

- Greek yogurt is made by straining yogurt and letting a liquid (called whey) drain out.
- This makes Greek yogurt thicker and creamier than regular yogurt.

Making Greek yogurt follows the exact same process as making regular yogurt, just with an extra step at the end: The yogurt is strained for several hours, just like you did in this activity. As the yogurt sits in the cheesecloth, a clear liquid called whey ("way") drains out. In this activity, you collected whey in the large bowl beneath the fine-mesh strainer.

No Whey!

Whey is made of water and proteins (called whey proteins). Straining out all that liquid leaves behind a thicker, creamier yogurt—Greek yogurt!—in the cheesecloth. And not to worry, the yogurt left behind is chock-full of other proteins called casein ("KAY-seen") proteins. Greek yogurt isn't the only strained yogurt out there. Skyr, an Icelandic yogurt, and labneh, a thick, creamy yogurt that's popular in the Middle East, are also strained.

For Good Measure

When we did this activity at the Recipe Lab, we started out with 2 cups of regular yogurt, minus the spoonful we tasted. After the regular yogurt sat in the cheesecloth overnight, we were left with just over 1 cup of Greek yogurt and just under 1 cup of whey. Add them together and you get 2 cups, the same amount of regular yogurt we started with. Because so much liquid is strained out, Greek yogurt manufacturers usually start with at least three times the amount of milk that regular yogurt manufacturers use!

Regular Yogurt

Greek Yogurt

Whey

PINEAPPLE-MANGO SMOOTHIE BOWLS

Yogurt gives these colorful, spoonable smoothie bowls their extra-creamy texture. But the key is choosing the right yogurt for the job!

SERVES: 2

TOTAL TIME: 20 minutes

LEVEL:

PREPARE INGREDIENTS

- 1 cup (5 ounces) frozen pineapple chunks
- 1 cup (5 ounces) frozen mango chunks
- ⅓ cup plain whole-milk yogurt
- ½ ripe banana, peeled and broken into pieces
- 2 teaspoons honey
- Pinch salt
- Toppings (see Make It Your Way, below)

GATHER COOKING EQUIPMENT

- Food processor
- Rubber spatula
- 2 serving bowls

START COOKING!

1. Add pineapple and mango to food processor and lock lid into place. Hold down pulse button for 1 second, then release. Repeat until fruit is finely chopped, about twenty 1-second pulses.

2. Remove lid and scrape down sides of processor bowl with rubber spatula. Add yogurt, banana, honey, and salt and lock lid back into place. Turn on processor and process until smooth, about 1 minute, stopping halfway through processing to scrape down sides of bowl.

3. Remove lid and carefully remove processor blade (ask an adult for help). Divide smoothie between 2 serving bowls using rubber spatula. Add your favorite toppings. Serve.

Goldilocks and the Four Yogurts

There are so many kinds of yogurt on the shelf at the grocery store, but which kind works best in a smoothie bowl? We tried Greek yogurt, but it was too thick and tart and gave the smoothie bowls a sour flavor. Low-fat yogurt and nonfat yogurt weren't creamy enough—using them makes for soupy smoothie bowls. But whole-milk yogurt was just right. When we used it in our smoothie bowls they turned out creamy and spoonable. Using plain yogurt is important, too—you want to be sure that you can taste the bright, sweet flavors of the fruit in your smoothie.

Make It Your Way

Toppings add even more flavor—and different textures—to your smoothie bowl. Try topping yours with **fresh berries, granola, sliced banana** or **kiwi, dried fruit,** or **nuts!**

MIXED BERRY MUFFINS

Thanks to some kitchen chemistry, the yogurt in the batter gives these muffins a lift in the oven! If the blackberries are large, cut them in half.

MAKES: 12 muffins

TOTAL TIME: 55 minutes, plus cooling time

LEVEL:

PREPARE INGREDIENTS

Vegetable oil spray

1 cup (7 ounces) sugar

1 tablespoon baking powder

½ teaspoon baking soda

½ teaspoon salt

3 cups (15 ounces) plus 1 tablespoon all-purpose flour, measured separately

1½ cups plain yogurt

2 large eggs

8 tablespoons unsalted butter, melted and cooled (see page 13)

1½ cups fresh or frozen mixed berries (blackberries, blueberries, raspberries) (do not thaw if frozen)

GATHER COOKING EQUIPMENT

12-cup muffin tin

3 bowls (1 large, 1 medium, 1 small)

Whisk

Rubber spatula

⅓-cup dry measuring cup

Toothpick

Oven mitts

Cooling rack

> **"I was surprised that I could use yogurt to make muffins! These are so good!"**
> —ANTONIO, 11

START COOKING!

1. Adjust oven rack to middle position and heat oven to 375 degrees. Spray 12-cup muffin tin with vegetable oil spray.

2. In large bowl, whisk together sugar, baking powder, baking soda, salt, and 3 cups flour. In medium bowl, whisk yogurt and eggs until smooth.

3. Add yogurt mixture to flour mixture and use rubber spatula to stir gently until just combined and no dry flour is visible. Gently stir in melted butter.

4. In small bowl, toss berries with remaining 1 tablespoon flour. Gently stir berries into batter. Do not overmix.

5. Use ⅓-cup dry measuring cup to divide batter evenly among muffin cups, using rubber spatula to scrape batter from measuring cup if needed (see photo, right).

6. Place muffin tin in oven. Bake until muffins are golden brown and toothpick inserted in center of 1 muffin comes out clean, 20 to 25 minutes.

7. Use oven mitts to remove muffin tin from oven and place on cooling rack (ask an adult for help). Let muffins cool in tin for at least 10 minutes.

8. Using your fingertips, gently wiggle muffins to loosen from muffin tin and transfer to cooling rack. Let cool for at least 10 minutes before serving.

What's Yogurt Doing in My Muffins?

Yogurt helps these muffins rise to the occasion. Yogurt is acidic—that's why it has a slightly tart or tangy taste. When the moist and acidic yogurt mixes with the baking soda in our muffin batter, it creates lots of bubbly carbon dioxide gas. In the oven, the liquid batter turns into solid muffins, and those tiny gas bubbles are trapped inside, giving these muffins their light, fluffy texture. Who says you can't eat your chemistry?

PORTIONING MUFFIN BATTER

Use ⅓-cup dry measuring cup to divide batter evenly among muffin cups, using rubber spatula to scrape batter from measuring cup if needed.

LUNCH, DINNER & SIDES

WHY DO ONIONS MAKE YOU CRY?

Onions are part of the genus of plants called alliums ("AL-ee-ums"). Just like you're related to your family at home, onions are related to all of the different kinds of plants and vegetables in the allium genus, such as shallots, garlic, leeks, and chives. In general raw onions are supercrunchy and very sharp—almost spicy—tasting. Some onions are slightly milder, mainly due to where they grow.

You can change the flavor of onions pretty drastically. With time and heat, cooked onions can be supersweet (see Caramelized Onions, page 52). With a hot vinegar bath, red onions turn supertangy (see Pickled Red Onions, page 54).

One thing all onions have in common? They can make you cry. What?! No, they aren't mean, and they won't make you sad. Check out our science experiment (page 49) to find out why, and find out how to prevent the tears.

FOR CRYING OUT LOUD

Chopping onions can make you cry—even if you're not sad! Find out why—and determine how to prevent tears—in this "emotional" experiment.

LET'S GO!

1 **MAKE A PREDICTION** In this experiment, you'll test 3 well-known techniques to prevent tears while chopping onions: holding a piece of bread in your mouth, wearing goggles, and soaking the onion in ice water before you chop it. Which technique do you predict will work best to prevent you from crying? Why?

2 Place 1 onion on cutting board. Use chef's knife to cut onion in half through root end (see photo, page 16). Lay onion halves flat on cutting board and trim tops, leaving root ends intact. Repeat with second onion (you'll have 4 halves total). Remove peels from onion halves. Discard peels. Leave onion halves cut side down until ready to use.

3 Add ice and water to 1 medium bowl. Place 1 onion half, cut side down, in bowl with ice and water. Let sit for at least 20 minutes.

4 Meanwhile, chop second onion half, following photos, page 16. Continue to chop onion repeatedly, using rocking motion and pivoting knife as you chop (make sure to rest fingers of your second hand on top of blade as you pivot and chop).5 Observe your results Did cutting this onion cause you to tear up? If so, was it a little bit, a lot, or somewhere in between? These results are your control that you can compare the next results to. Transfer chopped onion to second medium bowl and cover with plastic wrap. Leave the room for 5 minutes.

TOTAL TIME: 45 minutes

LEVEL: ▲

MATERIALS

2 yellow onions

Cutting board

Chef's knife

2 cups ice cubes

2 cups cold water

2 medium bowls

Plastic wrap

1 slice bread

1 pair swim, ski, or lab goggles

Paper towels

KEEP GOING! ↱

White
Onion

Vidalia
Onion

Yellow
Onion

Red
Onion

6 Hold slice of bread in your mouth. Repeat chopping with third onion half. Compare these results to the control: Did holding the bread in your mouth while chopping make your eyes tear more, less, or the same amount? Add chopped onion to bowl from step 5 and cover with plastic wrap. Leave the room for 5 minutes.

---

7 Put on goggles. Repeat chopping with fourth onion half. Compare your results to the control and to the bread technique: Did wearing the goggles while chopping make your eyes tear more, less, or the same amount? Add chopped onion to bowl from step 5 and cover with plastic wrap. Leave the room for 5 minutes.

---

8 When onion half in ice water is ready, remove from water and pat dry with paper towels. Repeat chopping. Compare your results to the control and the other techniques: Did soaking the onion in ice water before chopping it make your eyes tear more, less, or the same? Add chopped onion to bowl from step 5.

---

9 Cover bowl with plastic wrap and save chopped onions for another use. (Chopped onions can be refrigerated for up to 1 week. If a recipe calls for 1 chopped onion, use 1 cup.)

---

10 Compare the results of the three techniques you tried to the control. Which technique worked best to prevent crying while chopping the onion?

STOP UNDERSTANDING YOUR RESULTS
(Don't read until you've completed the experiment!)

THE BIG IDEAS

- Compounds produced when chopping onions are what make your eyes tear up.
- These compounds are created when the cell walls of onions break apart, which happens when you cut onions with a knife.
- Protecting your eyes with goggles keeps the compounds from reaching your eyes, so they won't create tears.

When we tried this experiment in the Recipe Lab, testers found that covering their eyes with goggles worked the best for preventing tears. Soaking the onion in ice water didn't do much (other than make the onions wet). Some testers said holding a piece of bread in their mouth made them tear up a little less—but most just felt pretty silly.

Have you ever noticed that whole onions, wrapped with their papery skins, don't smell much like onions? The most onion-y parts of an onion are compounds that aren't released until you start chopping or slicing. When you chop, slice, or mince onions, your knife breaks apart the tiny cell walls inside of the onion. This releases even smaller compounds trapped inside the onion's cells. Those compounds react to create some new compounds responsible for the pungent smell and taste of raw onion, and create others that can fly into the air and make your eye tear up to protect itself.

That's why wearing goggles worked the best in this experiment. Goggles block those harsh compounds from reaching your eyes, which prevents them from creating tears in the first place. (Simply wearing glasses or contact lenses works, too, though not quite as well.) The other techniques, soaking the onion and holding the bread in your mouth, don't protect your eyes. The theories were that soaking the onion would wash away some of the pungent tear-causing compounds and holding the bread in your mouth would . . . well, we're not really sure there.

The fresher the onion, and the more you chop it, the more new compounds are released—and the more you might cry! However, different people react differently to cutting onions. Some people are very sensitive and tear up a lot, and others aren't affected very much. This means that your results might be different from ours, depending on how sensitive you are.

CARAMELIZED ONIONS

With time, heat, and a bit of baking soda, onions can go from pungent to candy-sweet in just 40 minutes! Yellow or Spanish onions work best in this recipe. Sweet or Vidalia onions will taste too sweet, and red onions will turn too dark in color. If the onions look like they're burning instead of gently browning as they cook in step 6, turn the heat down a bit.

MAKES: About ¾ cup

TOTAL TIME: 40 minutes, plus cooling time

LEVEL:

PREPARE INGREDIENTS

- 1 tablespoon plus ⅓ cup water, measured separately
- ⅛ teaspoon baking soda
- 2 onions (about 1 pound)
- 1 tablespoon vegetable oil
- ¼ teaspoon salt

GATHER COOKING EQUIPMENT

Small bowl

Spoon

Cutting board

Chef's knife

10-inch nonstick skillet with lid

Oven mitts

Rubber spatula

Serving bowl

START COOKING!

1. In small bowl, combine 1 tablespoon water and baking soda. Use spoon to stir until baking soda is dissolved, about 30 seconds. Set aside.

2. Slice onions ¼ inch thick following photos, page 55.

3. In 10-inch nonstick skillet, combine onions, oil, salt, and remaining ⅓ cup water. Cook over medium-high heat until water is bubbling, about 2 minutes.

4. Cover skillet with lid and cook until water has mostly evaporated, about 5 minutes.

5. Use oven mitts to remove lid. Reduce heat to medium. Use rubber spatula to stir onions and gently press into bottom and sides of skillet. Cook, without stirring, for 1 minute.

6. Stir onions, scraping up browned bits from bottom and sides of skillet. Spread onions into even layer. Repeat gently pressing, cooking for 1 minute, and stirring until onions are softened, very brown, and look sticky, 12 to 15 minutes.

7. Add baking soda mixture to skillet and stir into onions. Cook, stirring constantly, until mixture has evaporated, about 30 seconds. Turn off heat.

8. Transfer onions to serving bowl. Let cool for at least 15 minutes. Serve warm or at room temperature. (Onions can be refrigerated in an airtight container for up to 3 days.)

Try It This Way

Caramelized onions are easily added to almost any meal. At breakfast, try them stuffed in an omelet or mixed into scrambled eggs. They taste fantastic on grilled cheese sandwiches, BLTs, and as a topping for burgers. Try sprinkling them on top of pizza or baked potatoes, or use them to jazz up plain mashed potatoes or rice.

Transform Your Onions

Raw onions are known for their sharp, fiery taste, but did you know that with enough time and heat, they become sweet? Cooking causes the onions to break down and soften, releasing water, sugars, and proteins. Over time, the water evaporates, concentrating flavor. Then, the sugars caramelize, which means that the sugar molecules break down and form hundreds of new flavor and aroma compounds that turn them brown. To boost this process even more, this recipe adds a little bit of baking soda at the end of cooking. The baking soda changes a flavorless compound in onions called inulin ("IN-you-lin") into fructose, which is a simple sugar and makes these caramelized onions taste even sweeter! Using this recipe, you can see onions transform from so pungent they'll make you cry to as sweet as candy in just 40 minutes!

recipe

PICKLED RED ONIONS

Onions don't always need to be cooked. A quick soak in a vinegar solution creates crunchy, tangy pickled onions—a great topping for tacos, burgers, or sandwiches.

MAKES: About 1 cup

TOTAL TIME: 40 minutes

LEVEL:

PREPARE INGREDIENTS

- 1 small red onion
- 1 cup white wine vinegar
- 2 tablespoons lime juice, squeezed from 1 lime
- 1 tablespoon sugar
- 1 teaspoon salt

GATHER COOKING EQUIPMENT

- Cutting board
- Chef's knife
- Medium bowl
- Small saucepan
- Fine-mesh strainer
- Jar with tight-fitting lid

> **"Easy and good. I love onions."**
> —TESSA, 11

START COOKING!

1. Slice onion into thin strips following photos, right. Place sliced onions in medium bowl.

2. In small saucepan, combine vinegar, lime juice, sugar, and salt. Bring to boil over high heat. Turn off heat.

3. Carefully pour vinegar mixture over onions (ask an adult for help—mixture will be VERY hot). Let mixture cool completely, about 30 minutes.

4. When mixture is cool, drain onions in fine-mesh strainer over sink, discarding liquid. Transfer to jar with tight-fitting lid or serve. (Pickled onions can be refrigerated for up to 4 days.)

Pretty in Pickled Pink (Red) Onions

These tangy, crunchy, punchy onions get their flavor from a process called pickling. Pickling means treating vegetables or fruits with acid so that they last longer before spoiling—in this case by soaking them in acidic vinegar. Raw red onions have deep purply-red skin and red-tinged white flesh. But, after a 30-minute bath in this vinegar mixture your red onions transform from deep purple to bright pink. It's all thanks to molecules called anthocyanins ("ann-though-SIGH-ah-nins") that are present in red onions (and lots of other colorful fruits and veggies such as cherries, red grapes, and blueberries). When acid interacts with anthocyanins, they turn red. Since vinegar and lime are both acidic, when this pickling solution comes into contact with red onions, the anthocyanins in the onion turn red, and you get sliced onions that are bright pink all the way through.

HOW TO SLICE ONIONS

1 Slice onion in half through root end, then use your fingers to remove peel.

2 Place onion halves flat side down on cutting board. Trim off ends and discard. Then slice onion vertically into thin strips, following grain (long stripes on onion).

WHY DOES FOOD TURN BROWN WHEN YOU COOK IT?

There's a simple truth when it comes to cooking: browned food is delicious.

It all comes down to chemistry—in particular, the Maillard ("my-YARD") reaction.

The Maillard reaction is something that takes place when food that contains both protein and sugars (think: steak, chicken, bread, and more) heats up. Starting around 250 degrees, the proteins and sugars begin to break down and combine, which creates not only browned color, but also hundreds of new flavor compounds. You can try this out yourself with Pan-Seared Strip Steaks (page 60), Ham and Cheese Panini (page 64), or even Roasted Cauliflower (page 62)—and explore how the Maillard reaction can change the flavor of butter in the science experiment on page 57.

BUILDING A
BETTER BUTTER

Lots of foods, from steak to chicken to pizza dough, taste better when they're golden brown. Is the same true for butter? Put your senses to the test and see if cooking butter until it turns brown changes its flavor. Use a regular, heavy-bottomed skillet in this experiment, because the dark color of nonstick skillets makes it hard to see when the butter is browned.

TOTAL TIME: 45 minutes

LEVEL: ▲

MATERIALS

10-inch skillet

8 tablespoons unsalted butter, cut into eight 1-tablespoon pieces

Rubber spatula

2 small bowls

1 blindfold per taster

1 plate per taster

1 glass of water per taster

1 slice white sandwich bread, cut in half, per taster

LET'S GO!

1 MAKE A PREDICTION Do you think melted butter and butter that's cooked until it turns golden brown (called browned butter) will taste the same or different? Why do you think so?

2 In 10-inch skillet, melt 4 tablespoons butter over medium-high heat. When butter is melted, reduce heat to medium-low.

3 Cook, stirring constantly and scraping bottom of pan with rubber spatula, until butter solids turn golden brown and butter smells nutty, 6 to 8 minutes (see photo, page 58). Turn off heat and carefully slide skillet to cool burner. Let skillet cool for 1 to 2 minutes.

4 Carefully pour browned butter into 1 small bowl (ask an adult for help), making sure to scrape out butter solids with rubber spatula. Set bowl aside. Wash and dry skillet and spatula.

KEEP GOING! ⤵

BROWNING BUTTER

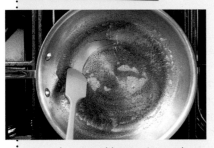

Your browned butter is ready when the butter solids (the specks at the bottom of the pan) turn golden brown and the butter smells nutty. Keep a careful eye on your skillet—butter can go from browned to burnt very quickly!

Eat Your Experiment!

Turn all of the butter from this experiment into a browned butter sauce! After step 11, add remaining plain melted butter to now-empty skillet. Brown butter over medium-low heat, following directions in step 3. Carefully pour browned butter in skillet into bowl with remaining browned butter from experiment (ask an adult for help). Add 2 tablespoons **lemon juice**, 2 tablespoons chopped **parsley**, and ½ teaspoon **salt** to bowl and use rubber spatula to stir to combine. Drizzle sauce over Roasted Cauliflower (see page 62) or Pan-Seared Strip Steaks (see page 60).

5 In clean 10-inch skillet, melt remaining 4 tablespoons butter over medium-high heat. When butter is melted, turn off heat and carefully slide skillet to cool burner. Let skillet cool for 1 to 2 minutes.

6 Carefully pour melted butter into second small bowl (ask an adult for help).

7 Choose 1 person to give out the samples for tasting (this is a good job for an adult). Everyone else will be tasters. Give each taster a blindfold, a plate, and a glass of water.

8 Explain that tasters are going to taste 2 samples of bread with melted butter. Their job is to focus on the butter and to notice if the 2 samples smell and taste the same or different. Tasters should keep their observations to themselves until everyone has finished tasting both samples.

9 Have tasters put their blindfolds on. Dip 1 piece of bread per taster into bowl of browned butter and place on each taster's plate. Tasters should smell the buttered bread and then eat it, taking small bites and chewing slowly. Have tasters take a few sips of water to give their tastebuds a break.

10 Repeat with remaining pieces of bread and bowl of plain melted butter. Ask if any tasters would like to repeat tasting with either sample.

11 **OBSERVE YOUR RESULTS** Have tasters remove their blindfolds. Ask tasters what they noticed about the 2 samples of butter. Did they smell similar or different? Did they taste similar or different? How so? Did tasters have a preference for either one?

STOP UNDERSTANDING YOUR RESULTS
(Don't read until you've completed the experiment!)

THE BIG IDEAS

- In many foods, heat triggers a chemical reaction between amino acids (the building blocks of proteins) and sugars that creates lots of new—and very delicious!—flavor compounds. It also creates other compounds that give browned foods their color. This is called the Maillard ("my-YARD"), or browning, reaction.
- Browning butter is one example of the Maillard reaction. As butter heats up, the water in the butter evaporates and sugars and amino acids in the butter react to create new flavor compounds and turn from white to brown.

Browned Butter

Melted Butter

In the Recipe Lab, we noticed a big flavor difference between the browned butter and the plain melted butter. Tasters reported that the browned butter smelled and tasted "nutty," "toasty," and "complex." The plain melted butter was, well, plain by comparison! Some tasters thought that the plain melted butter tasted sweeter than the browned butter. Were your results similar?

Butter is made of fat, water, and small amounts of sugar and protein. When you heat butter, its fat turns from a solid to a liquid as the butter melts. Once the butter reaches 212 degrees, its water boils and starts to evaporate. You probably noticed lots of bubbles in your butter—that was the water evaporating. As the butter continues to heat up, the magic begins: The butter's amino acids (the building blocks of proteins) react with its sugars to create totally new compounds, some of which are brown and many of which have new toasty flavors. This is known as the Maillard reaction or the browning reaction. It's named after Louis-Camille Maillard, the French scientist who first studied it in the early 1900s.

But the Maillard reaction isn't just for browned butter—lots of foods turn brown when they cook. Think steak with a dark crust (see page 60), golden-brown pizza crust, bronze roasted chicken, and more. And depending on the specific amino acids and sugars in a food, the Maillard reaction creates different flavor compounds. That's why browned beef tastes different from toasted bread, which tastes different than browned butter! Amazingly, even after a century of research, the Maillard reaction still isn't entirely understood by scientists—the chemistry is that complicated!

PAN-SEARED STRIP STEAKS

These steaks get their deliciously browned crust through the power of the Maillard reaction. You can also use rib-eye steaks for this recipe, if you prefer.

SERVES: 4

TOTAL TIME: 25 minutes

LEVEL:

PREPARE INGREDIENTS

2 (12-ounce) boneless strip steaks, about 1½ inches thick

1 teaspoon pepper

¼ teaspoon kosher salt

GATHER COOKING EQUIPMENT

Large plate

Paper towels

12-inch nonstick skillet

Tongs

Instant-read thermometer

Cutting board

Chef's knife

> **"I liked flipping the steak and taking the temperature."**
> —TY, 8

Here for the Sear

Pan searing is a great way to create a tasty crust on the outside of meat. The Maillard reaction begins on the surface of the meat, as it dries out in the heat of the pan. The proteins begin to break down into amino acids, and interact with the heat and sugars to create new flavor compounds (see page 59). The meat cooks from the outside in, so a layer of dark brown crust forms on the outside, while the inside stays pink. In this recipe, we start the steaks in a cold pan and flip them over every two minutes. This means that the meat's temperature rises gradually, allowing more time for nice browning to build up on the outside without overcooking the inside. (This slow start also keeps the steaks from smoking and splattering on the stove!)

START COOKING!

1. Place steaks on large plate. Use paper towels to pat both sides of steak dry; discard paper towels. Sprinkle steaks evenly with half of pepper. Flip steaks over and sprinkle evenly with remaining pepper.

2. Place steaks 1 inch apart in 12-inch nonstick skillet. Wash your hands. Turn heat to high and cook steaks for 2 minutes. Use tongs to flip steaks (see photo, right) and cook on second side for 2 minutes.

3. Reduce heat to medium. Flip steaks and continue to cook, flipping steaks every 2 minutes, until well browned and meat registers 120 to 125 degrees on an instant-read thermometer (see page 17 for how to use thermometer), 4 to 10 minutes longer. (Steaks should be sizzling gently in pan; if not, increase heat slightly. If skillet starts to smoke, turn heat down.)

4. Turn off heat and slide skillet to cool burner. Use tongs to transfer steaks to cutting board. Let steaks rest for 5 minutes. Use chef's knife to slice steaks crosswise (the short way) into thin strips (ask an adult for help). Sprinkle sliced steak evenly with salt. Serve.

FLIP FOR GOOD BROWNING

Use tongs to flip steaks over every 2 minutes until well browned and meat registers 120 to 125 degrees on an instant-read thermometer.

ROASTED CAULIFLOWER

Browning isn't just for meat! This roasted cauliflower is delicious served with Browned Butter Sauce (see page 58)—drizzle the sauce over the cauliflower on the platter in step 8, and do not use the extra 1 tablespoon oil or Parmesan cheese.

SERVES: 4

TOTAL TIME: 1 hour

LEVEL:

PREPARE INGREDIENTS

- 1 head cauliflower (about 2 pounds)
- 2 tablespoons plus 1 tablespoon extra-virgin olive oil, measured separately
- ¾ teaspoon kosher salt
- ¼ teaspoon pepper
- 2 tablespoons grated Parmesan cheese (optional)

GATHER COOKING EQUIPMENT

Rimmed baking sheet

Aluminum foil

Cutting board

Chef's knife

Oven mitts

Cooling rack

Tongs

Serving platter

START COOKING!

1. Adjust oven rack to lowest position and heat oven to 450 degrees. Line rimmed baking sheet with aluminum foil.

2. Pull and snap off outer leaves from cauliflower and discard. Trim and cut cauliflower into 8 wedges following photo, right. Transfer wedges to foil-lined rimmed baking sheet.

3. Drizzle 2 tablespoons oil over cauliflower wedges. Sprinkle evenly with salt and pepper. Use your hands to toss cauliflower wedges until evenly coated with oil and seasonings. Spread wedges into even layer, flat sides down, on baking sheet. Wash your hands.

4. Cover baking sheet tightly with aluminum foil. Place baking sheet in oven and roast for 15 minutes.

5. Use oven mitts to remove baking sheet from oven and place on cooling rack (ask an adult for help). Ask an adult to remove foil (be careful of steam!). Use tongs to flip wedges over (baking sheet will be hot!).

6. Use oven mitts to return baking sheet to oven and continue to roast, uncovered, until bottom sides of cauliflower are deep golden brown and cauliflower is tender, 12 to 18 minutes.

7. Use oven mitts to remove baking sheet from oven and place on cooling rack (ask an adult for help). Let cauliflower cool for 5 minutes.

8. Use tongs to transfer cauliflower to serving platter (ask an adult for help, baking sheet will be hot!). Drizzle with remaining 1 tablespoon oil and sprinkle with Parmesan cheese (if using). Serve.

HOW TO CUT CAULIFLOWER INTO WEDGES

Turn cauliflower on its side and use chef's knife to cut off stem. Turn cauliflower stem-side down on cutting board. Cut in half through middle of cauliflower. Place each half cut-side down on cutting board. Cut each half into 4 equal wedges on an angle through stem.

Two Steps to Perfectly Browned Cauliflower

We get a golden-brown crust without drying out the inside of the cauliflower by cooking the cauliflower in two stages. First by steaming, and then by browning. Cauliflower is made up of more than 90 percent water. When the cauliflower heats up in the oven, some of that water turns into steam. Covering the baking sheet with aluminum foil helps trap that steam so that the cauliflower can cook evenly. After you remove the foil, the steam escapes and the outside of the cauliflower starts to dry out. That's when the browning begins! Cauliflower contains proteins and sugars that, when subject to heat, begin the transformation called Maillardization (see page 59).

HAM AND CHEESE PANINI

Meat and vegetables aren't the only things that brown—bread turns toasty and delicious through the Maillard reaction, too (especially with the help of a little mayo!). Crusty slices of rustic bread are traditional in a panini, but hearty sandwich bread will also work in this recipe. If you have a nonstick grill pan, you can use it instead of the nonstick skillet—the pan will put grill marks on the sandwich, just like using a panini press!

SERVES: 1

TOTAL TIME: 20 minutes

LEVEL:

PREPARE INGREDIENTS

- 2 (½-inch-thick) slices crusty bread
- 1 tablespoon mayonnaise
- ½ cup shredded cheddar cheese (2 ounces)
- 1 slice deli ham
- 4–6 pickle chips, optional

GATHER COOKING EQUIPMENT

- Cutting board
- Butter knife
- 10-inch nonstick skillet
- Spatula
- Small, flat saucepan lid (smaller than skillet)
- Oven mitts
- Chef's knife

START COOKING!

1. Place bread slices on cutting board. Use butter knife to spread mayonnaise evenly over 1 side of each slice.

2. Flip 1 slice over (mayonnaise side down) and place in 10-inch nonstick skillet. Sprinkle evenly with half of cheese. Place ham and pickle chips (if using) on top of cheese. Sprinkle evenly with remaining cheese. Place second slice of bread on top (mayonnaise on the outside).

3. Heat skillet over medium heat and cook until bread is golden brown on bottom, about 4 minutes.

4. Use spatula to flip sandwich over (see photo, right). Place saucepan lid on sandwich and press down firmly, then leave lid in place (ask an adult for help, skillet will be hot).

5. Cook until second side is golden brown and cheese is melted, 1 to 2 minutes.

6. Turn off heat. Use oven mitts to remove lid. Use spatula to transfer sandwich back to cutting board. Let cool for 2 minutes. Use chef's knife to cut sandwich in half and serve warm.

HOW TO FLIP WITH EASE

Slide spatula completely underneath sandwich. Make sure to use a spatula large enough to hold sandwich. Carefully place fingertips on top of sandwich. Lift spatula and flip sandwich over, moving your fingers out of the way as you flip sandwich onto second side.

Mayonnaise . . . On the Outside?!

Lots of us put mayonnaise on the inside of our sandwiches . . . but not on the outside! Bread has both sugars and proteins and undergoes the Maillard reaction when heated (think, toast!). But you can help make it SUPER Maillard-y with the addition of mayonnaise. Mayonnaise is made from oil (a form of fat), egg yolks, acid (such as lemon juice or vinegar), a little bit of sugar, and sometimes a little bit of mustard. The proteins from the egg yolks plus sugar help spur along the Maillard reaction's browning and flavor building. So, the next time you want extra browning, reach for the mayo jar!

Make It Your Way

You can make this panini with lots of different cheeses, meats, or toppings! Try shredded **Monterey Jack cheese**, shredded **mozzarella cheesee**, or two slices of **provolone** or **Swiss cheese** instead of the cheddar, or sliced **deli salami**, **turkey**, or **roast beef** instead of the ham. For additions, try slices of **apple** or **tomato**, crumbled **cooked bacon**, or **Caramelized Onions** (see page 52) instead of the pickles. Use your imagination to make a panini creation of your own!

WHY DO SOME CHEESES MELT BETTER THAN OTHERS?

Cheese is one of the oldest foods. It's made, in different forms, all over the world. Most cheeses start in the same way: with milk. Milk is made up of water and milk solids, which include proteins, fat, and sugar. Cheesemakers help the milk solids in milk coagulate ("co-AG-you-late"), or group together, often with the addition of enzymes ("EN-zimes") called rennet. These bunches of milk solids are called curds. Curds—with the help of heat, time, and sometimes pressure—turn into cheese! Different cheeses are great for different purposes. Sometimes you want a SUPER melty cheese such as on your slice of pizza (see page 70) or in your saucy pasta (see page 74). Sometimes you want to add just a bit of intense cheesy flavor, and don't care about the meltability (see Frico Chips, page 170). Learn all about how cheese melts in our science experiment on page 67.

THE GOOEY SCIENCE OF
MELTING CHEESE

TOTAL TIME: 30 minutes

LEVEL:

MATERIALS

Cutting board

Chef's knife

1 (10- to 12-inch) flour tortilla

Rimmed baking sheet

Masking tape

Marker

2 tablespoons shredded mozzarella cheese

2 tablespoons shredded sharp or extra-sharp cheddar cheese

2 tablespoons shredded Parmesan cheese

Oven mitts

Cooling rack

Some cheeses melt into gooey deliciousness, while others turn greasy or grainy, or simply refuse to melt at all. Find out why in this (edible!) experiment. Don't use fresh mozzarella, mild cheddar cheese, or finely grated Parmesan cheese. You can swap the flour tortilla for corn tortillas or even small slices of bread.

LET'S GO!

1 Adjust oven rack to middle position and heat oven to 200 degrees.

2 Use chef's knife to cut tortilla into 3 equal wedges (see photo, page 68).

3 Arrange tortilla wedges on rimmed baking sheet. Use masking tape and marker to label baking sheet "Mozzarella" by left tortilla wedge, "Cheddar" by center tortilla wedge, and "Parmesan" by right tortilla wedge.

4 Sprinkle mozzarella in even layer on left tortilla wedge. Sprinkle cheddar in even layer on center tortilla wedge. Sprinkle Parmesan in even layer on right tortilla wedge (see photo, page 68).

KEEP GOING! ⤷

QUESTION 6
CHEESE

HOW TO PREP TORTILLAS

1 Use chef's knife to cut tortilla into 3 equal wedges.

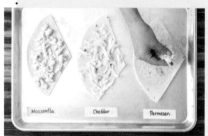

2 Sprinkle mozzarella in even layer on left tortilla wedge. Sprinkle cheddar in even layer on center tortilla wedge. Sprinkle Parmesan in even layer on right tortilla wedge.

Eat Your Experiment!

Snack on any (or all) of your cheesy creations. What do you notice about their flavor? Their texture?

5 **MAKE A PREDICTION** Do you think these 3 cheeses will melt the same way? Why do you think so?

_____

6 Place baking sheet in oven and bake for 10 minutes.

_____

7 Use oven mitts to remove baking sheet from oven and place on cooling rack (ask an adult for help).

_____

8 **OBSERVE YOUR RESULTS** Do the 3 melted cheeses look the same? In what ways do they look different? Which would you choose for your grilled cheese sandwich or pizza?

STOP UNDERSTANDING YOUR RESULTS

(Don't read until you've completed the experiment!)

THE BIG IDEAS

- Younger cheeses melt smoothly because they contain more water and a looser protein structure.
- As cheese ages, it loses water through evaporation, which also gives it a stronger flavor. Its proteins also bind more snugly to each other.
- Aged cheeses can leak fat when they melt or don't melt at all—but they can add lots of flavor to a dish.

Mozzarella   Cheddar   Parmesan

When we conducted this experiment in the Recipe Lab, our mozzarella melted into gooey perfection, our cheddar was melty but greasy, and our Parmesan didn't really melt at all. What were your observations?

The way a cheese melts has a lot to do with the cheese's age and how much water it contains. But before we get to that, let's talk about melting in general: Cheese doesn't melt the same way ice does—it doesn't go straight from a solid to a liquid. That's because ice is made of just one "ingredient" (water) while cheese is made up of a whole bunch of things, including protein, fat, and water.

Cheese is made of a network of proteins, like lots of tiny cages, surrounding bits of fat and water. When cheese heats up, the fat turns from solid to liquid. Then its proteins loosen up, which makes the cheese "flow" like a thick liquid.

As cheese ages, it loses water through evaporation (this also concentrates the cheese's flavor!). Cheeses with less water don't melt well because their proteins cling together tightly and they need more heat to melt. Plus, aged cheeses are less flexible when they melt. Instead of flowing smoothly, they squeeze out tiny droplets of fat. Parmesan is the oldest of our cheeses. It can be aged for more than one year and it barely melts at all, but it packs a TON of flavor. Sharp cheddar is our middle-aged cheese—it's aged for six to 12 months. While sharp cheddar does melt, it leaks greasy melted fat (this is called "breaking"). Mozzarella is our youngest cheese—it isn't aged at all, which means that it still contains lots of water and is excellent at melting. Young cheeses are your best choices if you're looking to add gooey melted cheese to your Skillet Pizza (page 70) or cheeseburger.

SKILLET PIZZA

Mozzarella gives this pizza its melty gooey topping while Parmesan adds a cheesy flavor kick. If your pizza dough is cold from the fridge, you can leave it out on the counter for 1 to 2 hours to bring it to room temperature before starting.

SERVES: 2 to 3

TOTAL TIME: 1¼ hours, plus time to make the dough, if making

LEVEL:

PREPARE INGREDIENTS

- 2 tablespoons plus 1 tablespoon extra-virgin olive oil, measured separately
- 1 (14.5-ounce) can whole peeled tomatoes, opened
- 1 garlic clove, peeled (see page 16)
- ½ teaspoon red wine vinegar
- ½ teaspoon dried oregano
- ¼ teaspoon salt
- ⅛ teaspoon pepper
  All-purpose flour (for sprinkling on counter)
- 1 pound pizza dough, room temperature (see Pizza Dough recipe on page 73, or use store-bought)
- 1 cup shredded mozzarella cheese (4 ounces)
- ¼ cup grated Parmesan cheese (½ ounce)

GATHER COOKING EQUIPMENT

Pastry brush	Liquid measuring cup
12-inch skillet with lid	Spoon
Colander	Oven mitts
Food processor	Cooling rack
Bowl	Spatula
Ruler	Cutting board
Rolling pin	Pizza wheel or chef's knife
Fork	

START COOKING!

1. Adjust oven rack to upper-middle position and heat oven to 500 degrees. Use pastry brush to paint bottom (not sides) of 12-inch skillet with 2 tablespoons oil. Set aside.

2. Set colander in sink. Pour tomatoes into colander. Shake colander and drain well.

3. Transfer drained tomatoes to food processor. Add garlic, vinegar, oregano, salt, pepper, and remaining 1 tablespoon oil. Lock lid into place. Turn on processor and process mixture until smooth, about 30 seconds. Stop food processor.

4. Remove lid and carefully remove processor blade (ask an adult for help). Transfer sauce to bowl and set aside.

5. Sprinkle clean counter lightly with flour. Place room temperature dough on floured counter. Shape pizza dough following photos, page 72.

KEEP GOING! ⤷

HOW TO SHAPE SKILLET PIZZA

1 Use hands to press dough into 6-inch circle. Use rolling pin to roll dough into 12-inch circle, rotating dough and reflouring counter every few rolls.

2 Place rolling pin on bottom edge of dough, then loosely roll dough around rolling pin. Gently unroll dough into skillet.

3 Using your fingertips, push dough into corners of skillet. Use fork to lightly poke surface of dough all over, about 10 times.

6. Use spoon to spread ½ cup sauce evenly over dough, leaving ¼-inch border around edge (save remaining sauce for another use). Sprinkle mozzarella and Parmesan cheese in even layer over sauce.

7. Cover skillet with lid and cook pizza over medium heat for 5 minutes. Turn off stove. Use oven mitts to remove lid.

8. Transfer uncovered skillet to oven (ask an adult for help). Bake until crust and cheese are spotty brown, 8 to 10 minutes.

9. Use oven mitts to remove skillet from oven and place on cooling rack (ask an adult for help—skillet handle will be VERY hot). Place oven mitt on skillet handle, so you remember handle is HOT, and let pizza cool in pan for 5 minutes.

10. Use spatula to slide pizza onto cutting board. Use pizza wheel or chef's knife to slice pizza. Serve.

Mozzarella: The Stretchiest Cheese

Why is mozzarella such a stretchy superstar? It has a lot to do with the way it's made. Adding acid or enzymes to milk starts the cheese-making process—it causes the milk to separate into solid curds and liquid whey. Those curds eventually get smooshed together into cheese. To make mozzarella, the cheese curds are stretched and pulled over and over again. During that stretching and pulling, proteins in the cheese make their way into very straight lines. When mozzarella is heated up, those straight lines of proteins loosen up and you can pull them into long strings. Other cheeses, such as Monterey Jack, melt really well (see page 69), but because their curds are pressed together, instead of stretched and pulled, their proteins don't form straight lines. When these cheeses melt, their proteins flow in lots of different directions, so the cheese doesn't stretch very much.

PIZZA DOUGH

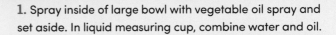

To measure ice water: Fill a large glass with ice and water and place glass in the refrigerator until you need it. Place the liquid measuring cup on a scale (if using) and tare the scale. Hold a fine-mesh strainer above the measuring cup. Pour the water through the fine-mesh strainer to measure the desired amount of water. Discard the ice.

MAKES: 1 pound

TOTAL TIME: 30 minutes, plus 1 hour rising time

LEVEL: ◼️ ◼️ ◼️ ▲

PREPARE INGREDIENTS

Vegetable oil spray

¾ cup (6 ounces) ice water

1 tablespoon extra-virgin olive oil

1⅔ cups (9⅛ ounces) bread flour

1 teaspoon instant or rapid-rise yeast

1 teaspoon sugar

1 teaspoon salt

GATHER COOKING EQUIPMENT

Large bowl

Liquid measuring cup

Food processor

Plastic wrap

1. Spray inside of large bowl with vegetable oil spray and set aside. In liquid measuring cup, combine water and oil.

2. Add flour, yeast, and sugar to food processor and lock lid into place. Hold down pulse button for 1 second, then release. Repeat until ingredients are combined, about five 1-second pulses.

3. Turn on processor, then slowly pour water mixture through feed tube and process until dough comes together and no dry flour remains, about 30 seconds. Stop processor. Let dough sit for 10 minutes.

4. Remove processor lid and sprinkle salt over dough. Lock lid back into place. Turn on processor and process for 1 minute. Stop processor.

5. Remove lid and carefully remove processor blade (ask an adult for help). Lightly spray counter and your hands with vegetable oil spray. Transfer dough to greased counter and use your greased hands to knead dough for 30 seconds, then form dough into smooth ball.

6. Place dough in greased bowl and cover with plastic wrap. Let dough rise until bubbly and doubled in size, 1 to 1½ hours.

Making Dough Ahead

To make dough ahead, let the dough rise (in the covered, greased bowl) in the refrigerator for up to 24 hours. About 2 hours before you use dough, take it out and let it come to room temperature.

recipe

SKILLET CHEESEBURGER MACARONI

SERVES: 4

TOTAL TIME: 50 minutes

LEVEL:

American cheese is the smooth-sauce-making cheesy star of this cheeseburger-inspired one-pot pasta! Make sure to use thinly sliced American cheese from the deli section of your grocery store in this recipe, not individually wrapped cheese "singles," which are made from different ingredients.

PREPARE INGREDIENTS

- 12 ounces 85 percent lean ground beef
- 1 small onion, peeled and chopped (see page 16)
- 2 tablespoons tomato paste
- 3 cups chicken broth
- 8 ounces (2 cups) elbow macaroni
- 2 teaspoons Worcestershire sauce
- 2 teaspoons dry mustard
- ½ teaspoon salt
- ¼ teaspoon pepper
- 8 ounces sliced deli American cheese, torn or chopped into pieces
- ½ cup chopped dill pickles (optional)

GATHER COOKING EQUIPMENT

12-inch skillet with lid

Wooden spoon

Oven mitts

> **"I liked it because it was chewy and gooey and the pickles added a nice crunch."**
>
> —BRANDON, 8

START COOKING!

1. Add ground beef, onion, and tomato paste to 12-inch skillet. Cook over medium-high heat, breaking up meat into small pieces with wooden spoon, until no longer pink, about 7 minutes.

2. Add broth, macaroni, Worcestershire, mustard, salt, and pepper to skillet. Use wooden spoon to stir to combine. Bring mixture to a boil over medium-high heat, stirring occasionally.

3. Reduce heat to low and cover skillet. Simmer until macaroni is tender, 8 to 10 minutes.

4. Use oven mitts to carefully remove lid from skillet. Sprinkle cheese evenly over mixture in skillet. Stir until cheese is fully melted and sauce is smooth (sauce may look loose but will thicken as it cools).

5. Turn off heat and slide skillet to cool burner. Let cool, uncovered, for 5 minutes. Stir in pickles (if using). Serve.

Where's the Milk?

Most recipes for macaroni and cheese build their creamy, cheesy sauce using a combination of milk; butter; flour; and, of course, cheese. This Skillet Cheeseburger Macaroni features a very creamy cheese sauce, but no butter or milk. Its gooey sauce is all thanks to one very special ingredient: American cheese.

Cheese is made of tiny droplets of fat and water, all held in place by a network of proteins (see page 69). When cheese melts, its fat (now a liquid) and its water separate, which makes many melted cheeses greasy and clumpy—not what we're looking for in our mac and cheese! American cheese contains special salts (called melting salts) which help keep the fat and water mixed—and our cheese sauce smooth. Melting salts are an example of an emulsifier—a special kind of molecule that helps fat (such as oil) and water mix. You can learn more about emulsifiers in Shake Things Up (page 121).

WHAT IS umami?

The five senses—touch, sight, sound, smell, and taste—are important when it comes to eating. In this question, we'll concentrate on taste. Humans can detect five different tastes: salty, sweet, bitter, sour, and umami ("oo-MA-me"). To understand umami, which is often described as "meaty" or "savory," first you need to understand how taste works.

As you eat, tastebuds inside your mouth and on your tongue tell you whether a food is sweet, sour, salty, bitter, or umami. Foods containing each taste stimulate tiny receptors in your mouth—kind of like puzzle pieces fitting together. Each taste has its own set of receptors: Salty foods trigger salt receptors, acids in sour foods trigger sour receptors, and so on.

Compounds called glutamates are responsible for fitting into the umami receptors in your mouth. You'll find meaty-tasting glutamates in meat, but you'll also find them in soy sauce, miso (page 81), tomato paste, nori (seaweed), cheese, and mushrooms (page 84). Can you detect the taste of umami? Try it out in our science experiment on page 77.

TOTAL TIME: 30 minutes

LEVEL: ▲

MATERIALS

Masking tape

Marker

3 bowls (1 large, 2 small)

Whisk

⅓ cup mayonnaise

¼ cup grated Parmesan cheese (½ ounce)

1 tablespoon lemon juice, squeezed from ½ lemon

1½ teaspoons Dijon mustard

1½ teaspoons extra-virgin olive oil

1 teaspoon Worcestershire sauce

1 small garlic clove, peeled and minced (see page 16)

⅛ teaspoon pepper

Pinch salt

Rubber spatula

1 anchovy fillet, rinsed, patted dry, and minced

1 blindfold per taster

1 small plate per taster

1 glass of water per taster

2 romaine lettuce leaves per taster

CAESAR'S
SECRET INGREDIENT

Something's fishy in this taste test! Can you identify the savory taste of umami by sampling two batches of Caesar salad dressing, one that includes an extra umami-packed ingredient and one without it? Then, use the rest of your dressing to make Caesar Salad (see page 78).

LET'S GO!

1 Make 2 masking tape labels. Use marker to write "A" on one label and "B" on second label. Place 1 label on each of 2 small bowls.

---

2 In large bowl, whisk together mayonnaise, Parmesan, lemon juice, mustard, oil, Worcestershire, garlic, pepper, and salt.

---

3 Use rubber spatula to divide dressing evenly between 2 small bowls. Add minced anchovy to bowl labeled "A." Whisk to combine.

---

4 **MAKE A PREDICTION** Do you think the two batches of dressing will taste the same or different? Why do you think so?

---

5 Choose 1 person to give out the samples for tasting (this is a good job for an adult). Everyone else will be tasters. Give each taster a blindfold, a small plate, and a glass of water.

KEEP GOING! ↷

A blindfold will help you to conduct a truly "blind" experiment!

Eat Your Experiment!

Use dressing to make Caesar Salad! Combine 2 small bowls of dressing into now-empty large bowl. Chop 2 **romaine lettuce hearts** (12 ounces) into bite-size pieces. Add chopped lettuce to bowl with dressing. Use tongs to toss to combine. Add 1 cup **croutons** and ¼ cup **grated Parmesan cheese**, and toss to combine.

6 Tasters should put on their blindfolds. Explain that they will taste two salad dressings. Their job is to decide whether the dressings taste the same or different and to describe the flavor of each dressing. Tasters should keep their opinions to themselves until everyone is finished tasting both samples.

7 Dip 1 lettuce leaf per taster into dressing in bowl labeled "A" and place on each taster's plate. Tasters should take small bites and chew slowly. Have tasters take a few sips of water to give their tastebuds a break.

8 Repeat with remaining lettuce leaves and dressing in bowl labeled "B." Ask if any tasters would like to repeat tasting with either dressing A or dressing B.

9 **OBSERVE YOUR RESULTS** Once everyone has finished tasting, ask tasters if the dressings tasted the same or different. How would they describe the flavor of the first dressing they tasted? The second dressing? Did one dressing have more umami—taste more savory—than the other? Which one? Did you like one dressing better than the other?

UNDERSTANDING YOUR RESULTS
(Don't read until you've completed the experiment!)

THE BIG IDEAS

- Umami is one of the five tastes, along with sweet, sour, salty, and bitter. The taste of umami is "meaty" or "savory."
- Compounds called glutamates ("GLUE-tuh-mates") are responsible for the taste of umami.
- When we eat foods that contain glutamates and other chemical compounds called nucleotides ("NEW-clee-oh-tides"), such as anchovies, it amplifies their umami taste—they taste even more savory.

In the Recipe Lab, tasters reported that dressing "A" (with anchovies) tasted more savory and had a deeper flavor than dressing "B." It turns out that a small fish can have a big impact on flavor. (And none of the tasters described dressing "A" as tasting fishy!) The savory taste they described is what's known as umami ("oo-MA-me"), which translates to "delicious" or "savory" from Japanese.

As we've learned (see page 76), the tastebuds in your mouth and on your tongue pick up the five different tastes—salty, sweet, bitter, sour, and umami.

Compounds called glutamates are responsible for the taste of umami, which is a meaty, savory taste. You'll find glutamates in meat of course, but also soy sauce, miso, tomatoes, Parmesan cheese, mushrooms and . . . anchovies!

Anchovies are extra-special in the umami department. They're not only chock-full of glutamates, but they also contain other chemical compounds, called nucleotides, that amplify their umami taste—talk about small but mighty!

The Caesar salad dressing you made in this experiment actually also includes two other umami-rich ingredients: Worcestershire sauce, which actually contains a small amount of anchovies, and Parmesan cheese. Take a tiny taste of each—do they taste savory to you? Try tasting other umami ingredients, such as tomato paste, miso, and soy sauce. What do you notice?

SALMON WITH MISO-ORANGE SAUCE

Miso is a thick paste made from fermented soybeans that's chock-full of savory umami taste—a perfect pairing with sweet orange and tender salmon.

SERVES: 4

TOTAL TIME: 40 minutes

LEVEL:

PREPARE INGREDIENTS

- ½ teaspoon grated orange zest plus ¼ cup orange juice, zested and squeezed from 2 oranges (see page 15)

- 3 tablespoons white miso

- 1 tablespoon packed light brown sugar

- 1 tablespoon unseasoned rice vinegar

- ¼ teaspoon cornstarch

  Pinch cayenne pepper (optional)

- ¼ teaspoon salt

- ¼ teaspoon pepper

- 4 (6- to 8-ounce) skin-on salmon fillets

GATHER COOKING EQUIPMENT

Small saucepan

Whisk

12-inch nonstick skillet

Tongs

Spatula

Instant-read thermometer

Serving platter

Spoon

START COOKING!

1. Add orange zest and juice, miso, sugar, vinegar, cornstarch, and cayenne (if using) to small saucepan. Whisk until smooth. Set aside.

2. In 12-inch nonstick skillet, sprinkle salt and pepper in even layer. Place salmon fillets, skin side down, in skillet. Wash your hands.

3. Cook salmon over medium heat, without moving salmon, until fat begins to puddle around fillets and skin begins to brown, 6 to 8 minutes.

4. Use tongs and spatula to carefully flip fillets (see photo, right). Cook, without moving fillets, until center of each fillet registers 125 degrees on instant-read thermometer, 6 to 8 minutes (see page 17 for how to use thermometer). Turn off heat. Transfer fillets, skin side down, to serving platter.

5. Bring miso mixture in saucepan to a simmer (small bubbles should break often across surface of sauce) over medium-high heat. Simmer, whisking occasionally, until thickened, about 1 minute. Turn off heat. Spoon glaze evenly over salmon. Serve.

HOW TO FLIP FISH

Gently slide spatula under fish to loosen skin from skillet, then use tongs to flip fish.

What Is Miso?

Miso is a thick paste made from fermented soybeans. Miso and its relatives have been essential ingredients in Japanese, Chinese, and Korean cuisines for thousands of years, adding savory umami taste to everything from soups to sauces to pickles. The first step in making miso is preparing a (friendly!) mold called koji ("KO-gee"). The koji is then mixed with cooked, mashed soybeans; salt; and sometimes water. That mixture sits for anywhere from a few weeks to a few years! Over time, the koji starts to break down the proteins, carbohydrates, and fats in the soybeans. It converts the soybeans' proteins into amino acids, including glutamatic acid, which give miso its trademark savory umami taste. At the same time, the koji turns the carbohydrates in the soybeans into simple sugars, which add some sweetness to the miso. According to the Japan Miso Promotion Board, there are 1,300 different types of miso!

PASTA WITH MEAT SAUCE

A secret ingredient makes this meaty sauce SUPER meaty tasting: mushrooms! If you don't own a food processor, you can chop the mushrooms and onions very finely by hand using a chef's knife. This sauce makes enough for 1 pound of pasta. If you want to serve only 8 ounces of pasta, use half the sauce and freeze the rest for up to one month.

SERVES: 4 to 6

TOTAL TIME: 1¼ hours

LEVEL: ▄▄ ▆▆ █

GATHER COOKING EQUIPMENT

Medium bowl

Rubber spatula

Cutting board

Chef's knife

Food processor

2 large pots

Wooden spoon

Colander

Ladle

Liquid measuring cup

Tongs

PREPARE INGREDIENTS

1 pound 85 percent lean ground beef

2 tablespoons water

1 teaspoon plus ½ teaspoon salt, measured separately, plus salt for cooking pasta

½ teaspoon baking soda

4 ounces white mushrooms

1 onion, peeled and chopped (see page 16)

1 tablespoon extra-virgin olive oil

3 garlic cloves, peeled and minced (see page 16)

1 tablespoon tomato paste

1 teaspoon dried oregano

1 (28-ounce) can tomato puree, opened

1 (14.5-ounce) can diced tomatoes, opened

1 pound pasta

¼ cup grated Parmesan cheese (½ ounce), plus extra for serving

START COOKING!

1. In medium bowl, combine beef, water, 1 teaspoon salt, and baking soda. Use rubber spatula to mix until well combined. Set aside.

2. Use chef's knife to trim and cut mushrooms following photo, page 84.

3. Add mushrooms and onion to food processor. Lock lid into place. Hold down pulse button for 1 second, then release. Repeat until vegetables are chopped fine, about eight 1-second pulses. Remove lid and carefully remove processor blade (ask an adult for help).

4. In large pot, heat oil over medium heat for 1 minute (oil should be hot but not smoking). Use wooden spoon to scrape mushroom mixture into pot. Cook, stirring occasionally, until vegetables are softened and well browned, 8 to 10 minutes.

5. Stir in garlic, tomato paste, and oregano and cook for 1 minute.

6. Carefully add beef mixture. Use wooden spoon to break up meat into small pieces.

KEEP GOING! ↻

HOW TO TRIM MUSHROOMS

Use chef's knife to trim off ends of mushroom stems and discard. Cut mushrooms in half if small or into quarters if large.

7. Carefully stir in tomato puree, diced tomatoes and their liquid, and ½ teaspoon salt. Use wooden spoon to scrape up browned bits on bottom of pot. Bring to simmer (small bubbles should break often across surface of mixture).

8. Reduce heat to low. Cook, stirring occasionally, until sauce thickens, about 30 minutes. Turn off heat.

9. Meanwhile, set colander in sink. Add 4 quarts water to second large pot. Bring to boil over high heat. Carefully add pasta and 1 tablespoon salt to pot. Cook, stirring often with wooden spoon, until pasta is al dente (tender but still a bit chewy), 10 to 12 minutes. Turn off heat.

10. Use ladle to carefully transfer ½ cup cooking water to liquid measuring cup. Ask an adult to drain pasta in colander. Return drained pasta to now-empty pot.

11. Stir Parmesan cheese into sauce. Add sauce and ¼ cup reserved pasta cooking water to drained pasta (ask an adult for help). Use tongs to toss until pasta is well coated with sauce. If needed, add remaining ¼ cup pasta cooking water, a little bit at a time, until sauce is loosened slightly and coats pasta well. Serve with extra Parmesan cheese.

We're Fond of You

Many meat sauce recipes begin by cooking chunks of meat until browned bits stick to the bottom of the pot. Those browned bits are called fond and they're absolutely packed with savory umami taste. But this recipe uses ground beef rather than chunks of meat, which will turn dry and pebbly if cooked long enough to create a fond. So we turned to mushrooms! Mushrooms are packed with umami flavor compounds, too. As you cook them they begin to brown and form flavor-packed fond on the bottom of the pot. Scraping up all that fond adds loads of umami flavor to your sauce. Bonus: Mixing the ground beef with baking soda helps keep it tender and moist.

WHY DO WE SALT OUR FOOD?

Salt is one of the most common ingredients in the world—you eat it, even if just a little bit of it, at every single meal. It is made of a compound called sodium chloride, which scientists abbreviate as NaCl. And it's powerful. Not only does it make food taste better, it can change the flavor, texture, and color of foods!

And salt is often on the move. It can move from a salty water bath into foods such as potatoes to both season the potatoes inside and out and make them creamier (see Salt-and-Vinegar Smashed Potatoes, page 90). It can pull water out of vegetables such as zucchini or carrots, preventing soggy sides (like Cheesy Zucchini–Carrot Crisps, page 92).

There are three main types of salt that we use in cooking. Table salt is what you'll see in salt shakers: very tiny, uniform grains of salt. Kosher salt comes in larger, coarser flakes. But not as large, coarse, or flaky as most sea salt, which often has a slightly more complex flavor due to the minerals present in the sea.

'TIS THE SEASON

TOTAL TIME: 1 hour

LEVEL: ▲

MATERIALS

2 quarts plus 2 quarts water, measured separately

Large saucepan

Masking tape

Marker

Serving platter

8 ounces plus 8 ounces green beans, measured separately, ends trimmed (see photo, page 88)

Large bowl

Ice

Colander

Dish towel

¼ cup table salt

1 plate per taster

1 fork per taster

Does boiling green beans in salty water change the way they cook? The way they taste? This experiment gives you the answer—and a side dish to eat!

LET'S GO!

1 **MAKE A PREDICTION** Do you think green beans cooked in salty water and green beans cooked in plain water will look the same or different? Will they taste the same or different? Why do you think so?

2 Add 2 quarts water to large saucepan. Bring to boil over high heat.

3 While water heats, make 2 masking tape labels. Use marker to write "Salted" on 1 label and "Unsalted" on second label. Stick labels on opposite ends of serving platter.

4 Add 8 ounces green beans to boiling water in saucepan. Return to boil and cook for 10 minutes.

5 While green beans cook, fill large bowl halfway with ice and cold water. (This is called an ice bath.) Place colander in sink. When beans are ready, carefully drain beans in colander (ask an adult for help).

KEEP GOING! ↪

HOW TO TRIM GREEN BEANS

To make trimming green beans easy, line up several green beans on cutting board and cut off tough ends. Do same thing on other end of beans.

Eat Your Experiment!

In small bowl, whisk together 3 tablespoons **extra-virgin olive oil**, 1 tablespoon **lemon juice**, ½ teaspoon **Dijon mustard**, and ⅛ teaspoon **salt**. Drizzle over all green beans. Use tongs to toss until well combined (mixing salted and unsalted green beans together). Serve.

6 Immediately transfer drained beans to ice bath. Let sit until no longer warm to touch, about 1 minute. Drain beans well. Transfer beans to dish towel and pat dry. Then transfer beans to side of serving platter labeled "Unsalted."

7 Add remaining 2 quarts water to now-empty saucepan. Bring to boil over high heat. Add ¼ cup salt and remaining 8 ounces green beans to boiling water in saucepan. Return to boil and cook for 6 minutes.

8 While salted green beans cook, return colander to sink and make second ice bath in now-empty large bowl.

9 When salted green beans are ready, carefully drain beans in colander (ask an adult for help). Immediately transfer drained beans to ice bath. Let sit until no longer warm to touch, about 1 minute. Drain beans well. Transfer beans to dish towel and pat dry. Then transfer to side of serving platter labeled "Salted."

10 OBSERVE YOUR RESULTS Invite your family and friends to join you for a taste test—don't tell them the difference between the green beans until after they taste! First, have everyone observe the two types of green beans. Then, have everyone taste a few of each type of bean. Have tasters keep their thoughts to themselves until everyone has observed and tasted. Ask tasters:

- How would you describe the color of each type of green bean?
- How would you describe the flavor and texture of each type of green bean?
- Do the two types of green beans taste the same or different?

STOP UNDERSTANDING YOUR RESULTS
(Don't read until you've completed the experiment!)

THE BIG IDEAS

- Cooking green beans in salty water seasons the beans inside and out thanks to a process called diffusion.
- The longer green vegetables cook, the duller their green color becomes.
- Green beans turn tender more quickly when they're cooked in salty water, which helps them keep their bright-green color.

Unsalted water
Bland, dull green beans

Salty water
Seasoned, bright green beans

Whoa! In the Recipe Lab, the green beans we cooked in salted water cooked in almost half the time—and stayed bright green!—compared to the beans we cooked in plain water. Plus, the saltwater beans tasted more seasoned and, well, green-beany. What about yours?

As vegetables cook, they become more tender and easier to chew, partly because the "glue" that holds plant cells together (called pectin) gets weaker. But something else happens as green vegetables heat up—they start to lose their bright green color. And the longer they cook, the duller and more drab their color becomes. Salt to the rescue! Adding all that salt to the cooking water is like pressing fast-forward on cooking the green beans. Salt weakens the pectin in green beans. This causes the green beans to become tender much more quickly. And less time in hot water means that these beans lose only a tiny bit of their bright green color.

Cooking green beans in salty water also seasons them, inside and out! Tiny molecules and ions, like the salt dissolved in the boiling water, naturally move from places where there are lots of them (the salty water) to places where there are fewer of them (the inside of a green bean). This process is called diffusion ("di-FEW-shun"). As the green beans cook in the salty water, some of the dissolved salt moves from the water into the green beans. This makes the beans taste what we call "seasoned." (Even though you added ¼ cup of salt to the water, only a tiny amount makes its way inside the beans.) This extra bit of seasoning brings out the flavor of the green beans. Thank you, salt!

recipe

SALT–AND–VINEGAR SMASHED POTATOES

SERVES: 4

TOTAL TIME: 1½ hours

LEVEL:

Cooking these potatoes in very salty water seasons them and makes them easy to smash. Use small red potatoes, measuring 1 to 2 inches in diameter. If you prefer to use kosher salt, you will need 1¾ cups of Morton kosher salt or 2½ cups of Diamond Crystal.

PREPARE INGREDIENTS

2 quarts water

1¼ cups salt

2 pounds small red potatoes

Vegetable oil spray

¼ cup extra-virgin olive oil

3 tablespoons malt vinegar

¼ teaspoon pepper

GATHER COOKING EQUIPMENT

Cooling rack

2 rimmed baking sheets

Large pot

Slotted spoon

Paring knife

Pastry brush

1-cup dry measuring cup

Ruler

Oven mitts

START COOKING!

1. Adjust oven rack to upper-middle position and heat oven to 450 degrees. Set cooling rack inside one rimmed baking sheet.

2. Add water to large pot and bring to boil over medium-high heat. Carefully add salt to water and stir with slotted spoon until dissolved.

3. Carefully add potatoes to pot (ask an adult for help). Cook potatoes until very tender, 20 to 30 minutes. To check if potatoes are tender, use slotted spoon to carefully transfer one potato to wire rack in rimmed baking sheet. Carefully insert paring knife into potato. If it slips in and out easily the potatoes are ready. Turn off heat.

4. Use slotted spoon to carefully transfer potatoes to cooling rack set in baking sheet. Let potatoes sit to dry out for 10 minutes.

5. Meanwhile, spray second rimmed baking sheet with vegetable oil spray. Use pastry brush to evenly coat baking sheet with olive oil.

6. When potatoes are dry, transfer potatoes to oiled baking sheet. Use 1-cup dry measuring cup to flatten each potato until ½ inch thick (see photo, above)

7. Use clean pastry brush to paint potatoes with half of vinegar. Sprinkle potatoes with pepper.

8. Place baking sheet in oven and roast until potatoes are well browned and crisp, 30 to 35 minutes.

9. Use oven mitts to remove baking sheet from oven and place on cooling rack (ask an adult for help).

10. Use pastry brush to carefully paint potatoes with remaining vinegar. Serve.

HOW TO SMASH POTATOES

Use 1-cup dry measuring cup to press down on each potato to flatten until ½ inch thick.

Supersalted Water

In this recipe, salt does double duty: not only does it give the potatoes their salty taste, but it also gives them their creamy texture. Just like in our experiment on page 87, there's a lot more salt dissolved in the supersalty boiling water than there is in the raw potatoes. As the spuds cook, some of that dissolved salt moves from the water into the potatoes, seasoning them all the way through. (Thanks, diffusion!) The salt also breaks down pectin in the potatoes (pectin is like a glue that holds the potatoes' cells together). As the pectin breaks down, the cells inside the potatoes start to separate. At the same time, lots of tiny starch granules in the potatoes' cells absorb water and swell up (think: teeny sponges), giving the potato a creamy (and smashable!) texture.

CHEESY ZUCCHINI-CARROT CRISPS

Harness the water-moving power of salt to make these CRISPS live up to their name. You can use a food processor with a shredding disk to shred the zucchini and carrot, if you prefer.

SERVES: 2 to 4
(Makes 12 crisps)

TOTAL TIME: 1 hour

LEVEL:

PREPARE INGREDIENTS

- Vegetable oil spray
- 1 small zucchini (6 ounces)
- 1 small carrot, peeled
- ½ teaspoon salt
- ⅓ cup panko bread crumbs
- ¼ cup shredded cheddar cheese (1 ounce)
- 1 large egg, cracked into bowl and lightly beaten with fork
- ½ teaspoon garlic powder

GATHER COOKING EQUIPMENT

- Rimmed baking sheet
- Parchment paper
- Cutting board
- Chef's knife
- Box grater
- Fine-mesh strainer
- Large bowl
- Rubber spatula
- Clean dish towel
- 1-tablespoon measuring spoon
- Oven mitts
- Cooling rack

START COOKING!

1. Adjust oven rack to upper-middle position and heat oven to 425 degrees. Line rimmed baking sheet with parchment paper and spray with vegetable oil spray.

2. Use chef's knife to trim off ends of zucchini and carrot. Shred zucchini and carrot on large holes of box grater (stop when your fingers get close to the grater and discard ends).

3. Set fine-mesh strainer over large bowl. Transfer shredded vegetables to strainer and sprinkle with salt. Use rubber spatula to stir until combined. Let sit for 10 minutes to drain.

4. Place clean dish towel on counter. When salted vegetables are ready, transfer to center of dish towel. Gather ends of towel together; twist tightly; and squeeze hard over sink, draining as much liquid as possible. Discard any liquid from large bowl and add vegetables to bowl.

5. Add panko, cheddar, egg, and garlic powder to bowl with vegetables. Stir mixture with rubber spatula until combined.

6. Use 1-tablespoon measuring spoon to scoop and drop vegetable mixture onto baking sheet in 12 mounds (about 1 heaping tablespoon each). Use your hand to gently press each mound to flatten into thin circle.

7. Place baking sheet in oven and bake crisps until edges are browned, 13 to 15 minutes.

8. Use oven mitts to remove baking sheet from oven and place on cooling rack (ask an adult for help). Let crisps cool for 10 minutes. Serve.

The Wizard of Os(mosis)

Vegetables and fruits such as carrots and zucchini (surprise— a zucchini is technically a fruit!) are mostly made up of water. (A zucchini or carrot is about 95 percent water.) It can be a challenge to deal with all that water when cooking or baking— no one likes soggy zucchini bread!

One of salt's many superpowers is that it can pull water out of food. Plants are made up of countless tiny cells. When you sprinkle salt on vegetables and fruits, some of the water inside the cells is pulled out toward the salt. This process is called osmosis ("oz-MOE-sis"). Squeezing the shredded zucchini and carrot in a towel gets some of the water out, but salting them and letting osmosis do its work lets you squeeze out double the water! So, for crisps that are crispy—not soggy—use salt to draw out that extra water before cooking.

WHY DO Spices HAVE SO MUCH flavor?

Without spices, our food's flavor would be very different. (Imagine cinnamon rolls without the cinnamon or a bowl of chili without the chili powder!) So, what are spices? Spices come from the dried bark, roots, seeds, and fruits of plants. Many spices are sold whole, such as dried cinnamon sticks, nutmeg, cardamom pods, and black peppercorns. Whole spices can be crushed and turned into powdery ground spices. Most of a spice's flavor comes from its aroma (smell). (Flavor is a combination of what we taste AND what we smell.) Our noses detect tiny aroma molecules that spices release into the air. Spices are packed with aroma molecules, which is why just a little bit of spice gives you a lot of flavor! In this chapter, explore how to unleash different elements of that flavor in a science experiment (page 95)—plus two recipes: Chicken Fajitas (page 98) and Chana Masala (page 100).

SPICES IN BLOOM

Spices are some of the most flavorful ingredients on the planet. Is there a way to take their flavor (and their fragrance) to the next level? Lots of recipes call for cooking spices in hot oil or butter before adding other ingredients. In this experiment, you'll heat a spice in oil and in water and then use your senses to observe whether the spice's smell changes.

LET'S GO!

1 Add 1½ teaspoons cinnamon to each of 3 small microwave-safe bowls. Add oil to 1 bowl of cinnamon. Add water to second bowl of cinnamon. Set aside third bowl of cinnamon.

2 Use 1 spoon to stir cinnamon-oil mixture until well combined. Use second spoon to stir cinnamon-water mixture until well combined and all cinnamon is wet, about 30 seconds (see photo, page 96). Set aside spoons, keeping track of which stirred oil and which stirred water.

3 **MAKE A PREDICTION** Do you think cinnamon heated in water will smell different from—or the same as—cinnamon heated in oil? Why do you think so?

4 Place bowl with cinnamon-water mixture in microwave and heat until boiling, 15 to 30 seconds (mixture should register about 200 degrees on instant-read thermometer, if using). Use oven mitts to remove bowl from microwave (ask an adult for help).

KEEP GOING! ↻

TOTAL TIME: 20 minutes

LEVEL:  ▲

MATERIALS

4½ teaspoons ground cinnamon

Measuring spoons

3 small microwave-safe bowls

2 tablespoons vegetable oil

2 tablespoons water

2 spoons

Instant-read thermometer (optional)

Oven mitts

1 blindfold per tester (optional)

STIR THINGS UP

You will need to stir the cinnamon-water mixture for longer than the cinnamon-oil mixture—make sure that all the cinnamon is wet!

5 Place bowl with cinnamon-oil mixture in microwave and heat until bubbling, 30 to 45 seconds (mixture should register about 200 degrees on instant-read thermometer, if using). Use oven mitts to remove bowl from microwave (ask an adult for help). (Microwaves primarily work by heating up water molecules in food. Fats, like oil, take longer to heat up in the microwave.)

6 Let both mixtures cool for 2 minutes. Stir both mixtures (using same spoons from step 2, use oil spoon to stir cinnamon-oil mixture and water spoon to stir cinnamon-water mixture) until well combined.

7 **OBSERVE YOUR RESULTS** Close your eyes—no peeking!—or put on your blindfold (if using one). Ask an adult or friend to hand you each of the 3 bowls (dry cinnamon, cinnamon-water mixture, and cinnamon-oil mixture), one at a time. Smell each bowl, taking a few deep, slow breaths in and out through your nose. In between bowls, take 3 long, deep breaths to give your nose a break.

8 What do you notice as you smell each bowl? Do the 3 bowls smell the same or different? How so? Do their smells remind you of anything, such as foods you've eaten?

STOP UNDERSTANDING YOUR RESULTS
(Don't read until you've completed the experiment!)

THE BIG IDEAS

- Most of a spice's flavor actually comes from its many aroma (scent) molecules.
- Some aroma molecules dissolve in water and other, different, aroma molecules dissolve in fat, such as oil or butter.
- When the water or fat is hot, the spices' cells break open, releasing even more aroma molecules into the liquid—and the air.

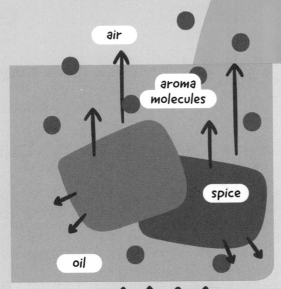

Here's what our spice smellers observed when we tried this experiment in the Recipe Lab: The dry cinnamon and the cinnamon-water mixture smelled "spicier," like "red hot candies." The cinnamon-oil mixture smelled "sweeter" and "more complex" and reminded one smeller of snickerdoodle cookies.

Let's unpack those observations. As you learned on page 94, most of a spice's flavor comes from its aroma (smell)—which is a huge part of flavor. Spices are packed with aroma molecules. Some aroma molecules dissolve when mixed with water, while most dissolve when mixed with fat, such as oil or butter. When the water or fat is hot, the tiny cells inside the spices break open, releasing even more aroma molecules into the liquid. Blooming spices—cooking them in hot oil or butter—releases different aroma molecules than heating spices in water. That's why the cinnamon-oil mixture smelled different than the cinnamon-water mixture. Blooming actually changes the flavor of the spice and the flavor of the butter or oil, too. And blooming works on more spices than just cinnamon: cumin, paprika, cayenne pepper, cardamom, nutmeg, and cloves, among others, all contain flavor molecules that dissolve in fat. Try repeating this experiment with one or more of those spices—what do you observe?

In Chana Masala (page 100), we bloom paprika, cumin, turmeric, ginger, and fennel seeds in vegetable oil. Smell the spices before you add them to the saucepan and again while they're cooking. Do you detect a difference?

recipe

CHICKEN FAJITAS

A sprinkle of spices turn plain chicken and veggies into flavor-packed fajitas. You can use a large green, yellow, or orange bell pepper instead of the red bell pepper. Serve fajitas with your favorite toppings, such as shredded cheese, sour cream, salsa, and guacamole.

SERVES: 4 (Makes 8 fajitas)

TOTAL TIME: 45 minutes

LEVEL:

PREPARE INGREDIENTS

- 1¼ teaspoons chili powder
- ½ teaspoon ground cumin
- ¾ teaspoon plus ¼ teaspoon salt, measured separately
- 4 (3- to 4-ounce) chicken cutlets (½ inch thick)
- 1 tablespoon plus 1 tablespoon vegetable oil, measured separately
- 1 large red bell pepper, stemmed, seeded, and sliced thin
- 1 onion, peeled and sliced thin (see page 55)
- 2 tablespoons chopped fresh cilantro (see page 15)
- 1 tablespoon lime juice, squeezed from 1 lime, plus limes wedges for serving (see page 15)
- 8 (8-inch) flour tortillas

GATHER COOKING EQUIPMENT

- Small bowl
- Spoon
- 2 plates (1 large, 1 large microwave-safe)
- Paper towels
- 12-inch nonstick skillet with lid
- Tongs
- Cutting board
- Aluminum foil
- Wooden spoon
- Oven mitts
- Serving platter
- Chef's knife
- Dish towel

START COOKING!

1. In small bowl, combine chili powder, cumin, and ¾ teaspoon salt. Use spoon to stir spices until well combined.

2. Place chicken cutlets on large plate. Pat chicken dry with paper towels. Sprinkle spice mixture evenly over both sides of chicken. Wash your hands.

3. In 12-inch nonstick skillet, heat 1 tablespoon oil over medium-high heat for 1 minute (oil should be hot but not smoking). Use tongs to carefully add chicken cutlets to skillet. Cook until lightly browned, about 3 minutes.

4. Use clean tongs to flip chicken cutlets. Cook until second side is browned and chicken is cooked (see photo, below), about 3 minutes. Turn off heat and slide skillet to cool burner.

5. Use clean tongs to transfer chicken cutlets to cutting board. Cover chicken cutlets with aluminum foil.

6. Add bell pepper, onion, remaining ¼ teaspoon salt, and remaining 1 tablespoon oil to now-empty skillet. Use wooden spoon to stir to combine. Cover and cook over medium-high heat until vegetables are brown on bottoms, about 4 minutes.

7. Use oven mitts to carefully remove lid. Stir vegetables, then cook until vegetables are soft and spotty brown all over, 3 to 5 minutes. Turn off heat and slide skillet to cool burner. Stir cilantro and lime juice into vegetables in skillet. Transfer vegetables to serving platter.

8. Slice chicken cutlets diagonally into thin strips. Use tongs to transfer sliced chicken to serving platter with vegetables.

9. Stack tortillas on microwave-safe plate, and cover with damp dish towel. Heat in microwave until warm, about 1 minute. Serve chicken and vegetables with warm tortillas, lime wedges, and your favorite toppings.

Nice and Spiced

Fajitas ("fah-HEE-tas") are a type of Texan-Mexican (Tex-Mex) food, which began in the mid-1800s with the cuisine of people of Mexican heritage living in Texas and people living in northern Mexico near the Texas border. To give the chicken in these fajitas a ton of flavor, we season them with two spices: cumin and chili powder. Cumin is the dried seed of a plant that's related to parsley. Today, you'll find cumin in dishes from around the world, such as palak dal (a lentil stew) from northern India; chelow (a rice dish) from Iran; stir-fried beef from Hunan, China; Tex-Mex chili; and more. Chili powder is a blend of spices—it usually includes dried, ground chile peppers, oregano, garlic powder, and even a bit of cumin. Depending on the kinds of chiles used, chili powder can be mild or spicy. In addition to fajitas, you'll always find chili powder in recipes for—you guessed it—chili!

COOKING CHICKEN THROUGH

Use a chef's knife to cut into the thickest part of the chicken cutlet. If it's opaque (you can't see through it), it's fully cooked.

recipe

CHANA MASALA

Six different spices give these chickpeas lots of flavor—without being spicy! Serve Chana Masala with rice, naan, and/or lime wedges. If you use low-sodium chickpeas, increase the salt to ¾ teaspoon.

SERVES: 4 to 6

TOTAL TIME: 1 hour and 10 minutes

LEVEL:

PREPARE INGREDIENTS

10 sprigs cilantro

 1 small onion, peeled and chopped (see page 16)

 2 garlic cloves, peeled and chopped (see page 16)

 1 (14.5-ounce) can whole peeled tomatoes, opened

 3 tablespoons vegetable oil

 1 teaspoon paprika

 1 teaspoon ground cumin

 ½ teaspoon ground turmeric

 ½ teaspoon ground ginger

 ½ teaspoon fennel seeds

 2 (15-ounce) cans chickpeas, opened (do not drain)

1½ teaspoons garam masala

 ½ teaspoon salt

GATHER COOKING EQUIPMENT

Cutting board

Chef's knife

Food processor

Wooden spoon

Large saucepan with lid

Oven mitts

START COOKING!

1. Pick cilantro leaves off stems and separate stems and leaves. Use chef's knife to chop leaves; set aside for serving. Cut stems into 1-inch pieces.

2. Add cilantro stems, onion, and garlic to food processor and lock lid into place. Turn on processor and process until vegetables are finely chopped, about 10 seconds. Stop processor.

3. Remove lid and carefully remove processor blade (ask an adult for help). Use wooden spoon to scrape onion mixture into large saucepan. Set aside.

4. Replace blade in now-empty food processor (ask an adult for help). Add tomatoes and their liquid to processor and lock lid into place. Turn on processor and process until tomatoes are smooth, about 30 seconds. Stop processor. Remove lid and carefully remove food processor blade (ask an adult for help). Set aside.

5. Add oil to onion mixture in saucepan. Cook over medium-high heat, stirring often, until onions are softened and beginning to brown, 5 to 7 minutes.

6. Add paprika, cumin, turmeric, ginger, and fennel seeds to onion mixture. Cook, stirring constantly, for 1 minute.

7. Stir in chickpeas and their liquid and processed tomatoes. Use wooden spoon to scrape up browned bits on bottom of saucepan. Bring mixture to boil.

8. Reduce heat to medium-low. Cover saucepan with lid and simmer (small bubbles should break often across surface of sauce) for 15 minutes.

9. Use oven mitts to remove lid. Stir garam masala and salt into chickpeas. Continue to cook, uncovered and stirring occasionally, until sauce has thickened, 10 to 12 minutes. Turn off heat. Serve, sprinkling individual portions with reserved chopped cilantro leaves.

Masala Magic

In Indian cooking, "masala" means "blend." Many Indian home cooks have a masala dabba—a large container with smaller containers inside, each filled with a different spice. Cooks mix and match the spices to flavor a wide variety of recipes. Some of these spice combinations are so common that they have their own names, such as garam masala, which means "warm spice blend." Different regions, and even different families, have their own combinations of spices in their garam masala blends, which often include black pepper, coriander, cardamom, cumin, and cinnamon.

In this recipe, most of the spices are added at the beginning of cooking. Blooming these spices in the hot oil brings out some of their flavor compounds and flavors the oil, too (see page 97). As the spices simmer, their aroma mellows, providing much of the sauce's background flavor. The garam masala, however, isn't added to the saucepan until later. This helps garam masala's spices keep more of their aromas (as spices cook for a long time, they lose some of their smell). It also means that you get to enjoy more of their flavor as you eat your Chana Masala!

WHY DO DIFFERENT PARTS OF THE CHICKEN TASTE AND LOOK DIFFERENT?

White meat, dark meat—what's the difference? Chickens have dark meat in the parts of the bird that get a lot of exercise (thighs!). The meat is darker in color because it contains more of the protein myoglobin ("MY-oh-globe-in"), which helps store oxygen in muscle cells that are important for movement. Dark meat also contains more fat and connective tissue, and needs to be cooked for a long time for a tender finished dish such as our Chicken Tinga Tacos (page 106). Chickens have white meat in the parts that don't get as much exercise (breasts!). Because it has less fat and connective tissue, white meat doesn't hold on to moisture as well. It can get pretty dry when cooked. To keep chicken breasts juicy we often brine them and cook them quickly. See for yourself in our science experiment (page 103) and Tiny Chicken Tenders (page 108).

A MYSTERY TO DISSOLVE

TOTAL TIME: 1¼ hours

LEVEL:

MATERIALS

Masking tape

Marker

2 large plates

Paper towels

Cutting board

Large bowl

Whisk

2 quarts water

½ cup table salt

4 (6- to 8-ounce) boneless, skinless chicken breasts

¼ teaspoon pepper

10-inch nonstick skillet

1 tablespoon plus 1 tablespoon extra-virgin olive oil, measured separately

Tongs

Instant-read thermometer

Aluminum foil

Chef's knife

1 plate per taster

1 fork per taster

Is there a way to turn chicken breasts, which are made of white meat and get a bad rap for being "boring," into a juicy, seasoned part of your lunch or dinner? Put your tastebuds to the test—and cook a meal for your family—in this edible experiment.

LET'S GO!

1 Make 2 masking tape labels. Use marker to write "Brined" on 1 label and "Unbrined" on second label. Stick 1 label on each large plate. Line both plates with paper towels.

2 Make 2 more masking tape labels. Use marker to write "Brined" on 1 label and "Unbrined" on second label. Stick labels on opposite ends of cutting board.

3 In large bowl, whisk water and salt until salt dissolves. (This mixture of salt and water is called a brine.)

4 Place 2 chicken breasts in brine and refrigerate for 30 minutes. Wash your hands.

5 **MAKE A PREDICTION** Do you think brined chicken and unbrined chicken will taste the same or different after they're cooked? Why do you think so?

6 Remove chicken from brine and place on paper towel–lined plate labeled "Brined." Discard brine in sink. Use more paper towels to pat chicken dry all over (see photo, page 104).

KEEP GOING! ↷

HOT TO PAT CHICKEN DRY

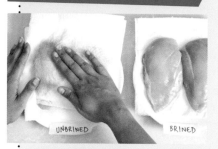

Place brined chicken breasts on large plate labeled "Brined" and remaining 2 chicken breasts on plate labeled "Unbrined." Use paper towels to pat chicken breasts all over until dry.

Eat Your Experiment!

Serve remaining chicken for lunch or dinner with your favorite sauce, such as **barbecue sauce**, **teriyaki sauce**, or **chimichurri sauce**. You can also slice chicken breasts and add them to tacos, sandwiches, or salads.

7 Place remaining 2 chicken breasts on large plate labeled "Unbrined" and use paper towels to pat dry all over. Sprinkle pepper evenly over both sides of all 4 chicken breasts. Wash your hands.

8 In 10-inch nonstick skillet, heat 1 tablespoon oil over medium heat for 1 minute (oil should be hot but not smoking). Use tongs to carefully place 2 unbrined chicken breasts in skillet. Cook until browned on first side, 6 to 8 minutes.

9 Use clean tongs to flip chicken breasts and cook until chicken registers 165 degrees on instant-read thermometer, 6 to 8 minutes (see page 17, and ask an adult for help). Turn off heat.

10 Use clean tongs to transfer cooked chicken to "Unbrined" side of cutting board. Cover chicken with aluminum foil.

11 Repeat cooking in steps 8 and 9 with remaining 1 tablespoon oil and remaining 2 brined chicken breasts. Transfer chicken to "Brined" side of cutting board and let rest for 5 minutes.

12 **OBSERVE YOUR RESULTS** Slice 1 unbrined chicken breast and 1 brined chicken breast. Invite your family and friends to join you for a taste test— don't tell them the difference between the chicken breasts until after they taste! Give each taster a plate and fork and have everyone taste a few bites of the unbrined and brined chicken. Have tasters keep their thoughts to themselves until everyone has finished tasting. Ask tasters:

• How would you describe the flavor of each type of chicken? Do they taste the same or different?
• How would you describe the texture of each type of chicken? Are they the same or different?

STOP UNDERSTANDING YOUR RESULTS
(Don't read until you've completed the experiment!)

THE BIG IDEAS

- Chicken breasts don't contain much fat, so they can be bland and dry when they're cooked.
- Through diffusion and osmosis, salt and water move from the brine into the chicken breasts, making them juicy, tender, and seasoned all the way through.

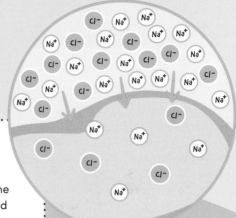

The dissolved salt travels from the brine into the chicken, seasoning it and changing the shape of its proteins.

When we did this experiment in the Recipe Lab, our volunteer tasters reported that the brined chicken breasts were more flavorful and juicy and that they tasted evenly seasoned in every bite. They noted that the unbrined chicken tasted plain and a "little dry." What did your tasters think?

When it comes to food, fat usually means flavor. Chicken breasts, often referred to as "white meat," don't contain much fat, so they can easily taste pretty bland and dry. Luckily, if you have some salt on hand, you can turn chicken breasts from meh to moist. Salt's superpowers (for more on salt, see page 86) transform chicken—and just about any other meat—in two different ways: Tiny molecules and ions (such as the salt dissolved in the brine) naturally move from places where there are a lot of them to places where there are fewer of them. This is called diffusion ("di-FEW-shun"). The brine contains more salt than the chicken. As the chicken sits in the brine, some salt moves from the brine into the chicken. This makes the chicken taste more seasoned.

Water also travels around during chicken's bath in the brine—water moves from the brine (where there's a lot of it!) to the inside of the chicken (where there's less of it). This process is called osmosis ("oz-MOE-sis") and it makes brined meat juicier than unbrined meat. But water alone doesn't make meat juicy, you need salt to save the day. When the salt in the brine travels into the chicken, it changes the shape of the protein molecules in the meat. This helps the chicken hold on to its added water, even after it's cooked, and it makes the meat more tender, too. Brining, it's a win-win!

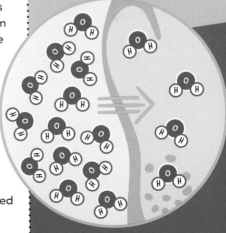

Water moves from the brine into the chicken, making it even juicier.

TACOS DE TINGA DE POLLO

(CHICKEN TINGA TACOS)

Slowly cooking chicken thighs in a smoky tomato sauce turns them into a tender taco filling. Serve with your favorite toppings, such as cilantro, cotija cheese, and Pickled Red Onions (see page 54).

SERVES: 4
(Makes 8 to 10 tacos)

TOTAL TIME: 1¼ hours

LEVEL:

PREPARE INGREDIENTS

- 2 tablespoons vegetable oil
- 1 onion, peeled and chopped fine (see page 16)
- 3 garlic cloves, peeled and minced (see page 16)
- 1 teaspoon salt
- 1 teaspoon ground cumin
- ½ teaspoon smoked paprika
- ¼ teaspoon ground cinnamon
- ⅛–¼ teaspoon chipotle chile powder
- 1 (8-ounce) can tomato sauce, opened
- 1½ pounds boneless, skinless chicken thighs
- 1 teaspoon grated lime zest plus 1 tablespoon lime juice, zested and squeezed from 1 lime (see page 15)
- 8–10 (6-inch) corn tortillas

GATHER COOKING EQUIPMENT

Large saucepan with lid

Wooden spoon

Tongs

Oven mitts

2 plates (1 large, 1 microwave-safe)

2 forks

Dish towel

START COOKING!

1. In large saucepan, heat oil over medium heat for 1 minute (oil should be hot but not smoking). Add onion and cook, stirring occasionally with wooden spoon, until lightly browned, 5 to 7 minutes.

2. Stir in garlic, salt, cumin, paprika, cinnamon, and chipotle chile powder and cook until fragrant, about 30 seconds.

3. Stir in tomato sauce, scraping up any browned bits on bottom of saucepan. Use tongs to add chicken to saucepan and stir to combine.

4. Bring mixture to boil. Reduce heat to medium-low; cover; and cook until chicken is very tender, about 25 minutes. Turn off heat.

5. Use oven mitts to remove lid. Use clean tongs to transfer chicken to large plate and let cool slightly. Use 2 forks to shred chicken into bite-size pieces (see photo, right).

6. Return shredded chicken to saucepan. Cook over medium heat, stirring often with wooden spoon, until sauce thickens and clings to chicken, 10 to 15 minutes. Turn off heat. Stir in lime zest and juice.

7. Stack tortillas on microwave-safe plate and cover with damp dish towel. Heat in microwave until warm, about 1 minute. Divide chicken evenly among warmed tortillas. Serve.

Praise for the Braise

These tacos are made with chicken thighs, which are dark meat. Because dark meat contains a lot of connective tissue (chewy bundles of proteins called collagen), we need to cook it for a long time to turn it from tough to tender. Simmering meat with a small amount of liquid in a covered pot for a long time is a technique is called braising. Braising creates extra-tender, moist meat. Plus, the liquid picks up flavor from the meat and can become a superflavorful sauce. In this recipe, we braise chicken thighs in the simmering sauce for about 25 minutes, until they're so tender that you can easily shred them with a fork. When all that collagen breaks down (into gelatin proteins, which are great at absorbing water and forming a succulent, juicy sauce when they do), you're left with moist, tender, shreddable meat and a savory spiced sauce, ready to fill your tortillas!

HOW TO SHRED MEAT

Use 2 forks to pull meat apart and shred it into bite-size pieces.

TINY CHICKEN TENDERS

Brining chicken breasts in a salt and sugar solution makes sure our baked nuggets are tender, juicy, and perfectly seasoned!

SERVES: 3 to 4
(Makes 18 nuggets)

TOTAL TIME: 1½ hours

LEVEL:

GATHER COOKING EQUIPMENT

Rimmed baking sheet

Aluminum foil

2 cooling racks

2 bowls (1 large, 1 medium microwave-safe)

Whisk

Cutting board

Chef's knife

Rubber spatula

Oven mitts

Shallow dish

Large plate

Paper towels

Slotted spoon

PREPARE INGREDIENTS

Vegetable oil spray

4 cups water

2 tablespoons sugar

2 tablespoons plus ½ teaspoon salt, measured separately

2 (8-ounce) boneless, skinless chicken breasts

1½ cups panko bread crumbs

3 tablespoons extra-virgin olive oil

2 large eggs

2 tablespoons all-purpose flour

2 teaspoons onion powder

½ teaspoon garlic powder

¼ teaspoon pepper

START COOKING!

1. Adjust oven rack to middle position and heat oven to 400 degrees. Line rimmed baking sheet with aluminum foil and set one cooling rack inside baking sheet. Spray rack with vegetable oil spray.

2. In large bowl, combine water, sugar, and 2 tablespoons salt. Whisk until sugar and salt are dissolved.

3. Place chicken on cutting board. Use chef's knife to cut each breast diagonally into three roughly equal pieces, then cut each piece crosswise into three even pieces (see photo, page 110).

4. Add chicken to water mixture in bowl. Wash your hands. Let sit for 15 minutes.

5. Meanwhile, in medium microwave-safe bowl, combine panko and oil. Use rubber spatula to toss bread crumbs to coat evenly with oil. Heat in microwave for 30 seconds. Use oven mitts to remove bowl from microwave.

6. Use rubber spatula to stir bread crumbs, scraping bottom of bowl. Return bowl to microwave and heat until light golden brown, 2 to 3 minutes longer, stopping to stir and scrape bottom of bowl every 30 seconds.

KEEP GOING! ↷

HOW TO CUT CHICKEN INTO TENDERS

Place chicken on cutting board. Use chef's knife to cut each breast diagonally into three roughly equal pieces, then cut each piece crosswise into three even pieces.

7. Use oven mitts to remove bowl from microwave. Let cool slightly.

8. In shallow dish, whisk together eggs, flour, onion powder, garlic powder, pepper, and remaining ½ teaspoon salt.

9. Line large plate with paper towels. When chicken is ready, use slotted spoon to remove chicken from brine and place on paper towel–lined plate. Discard brine in sink. Use more paper towels to pat chicken dry all over.

10. Dredge chicken pieces in egg mixture, followed by bread crumb mixture (following photos, page 111). Place coated chicken pieces on greased rack in rimmed baking sheet. Wash your hands.

11. Place baking sheet in oven and bake until chicken is crisp and cooked through (see photo, page 99), 15 to 20 minutes.

12. Use oven mitts to remove baking sheet from oven and place on second cooling rack (ask an adult for help). Let cool for 5 minutes. Serve.

> *"I got to work by myself. I would give it ten million stars!"*
> —CHARLOTTE, 8

1 Working with 3 to 4 pieces of chicken at a time, use your hands to add chicken pieces to shallow dish with egg mixture. Turn pieces, making sure all sides are coated.

2 Let excess egg mixture drip off before transferring chicken pieces to second bowl with bread crumb mixture. Toss chicken to coat all sides evenly with bread crumbs, pressing gently so bread crumbs stick to chicken.

3 Place coated chicken pieces on greased rack in rimmed baking sheet. Repeat with remaining pieces of chicken.

The Secret to Juicy Tenders

These tenders are made with chicken breasts (white meat), which are lighter in color and can get pretty dry when cooked, if you're not careful (see page 102). The solve? A saltwater solution, also known as a brine. As the chicken breast pieces soak in the brine, some salt and water move from the brine into the chicken, which both seasons the chicken and makes it more tender and juicy (see page 105 for the salty science). The salt in the brine changes the shape of the proteins in the meat as it moves into the chicken. This helps the chicken hold on to its water, even after cooking, and makes the meat more tender. A white meat win!

HOW DOES pasta cook?

Noodles are used in cuisines around the world. They're a simple food, made from flour and water and, often, eggs. While different cultures use different types of flour and different cooking techniques, for this question, we're concentrating on dried Italian-style pasta. Most pastas start out hard and dry and need both heat and water to cook. As they cook in boiling water, the noodles absorb some of that water and become softer and more flexible. Dry pasta baked in the oven would never get soft, and pasta soaked in cold water would become rubbery (its starch needs heat to gel!). Explore the power of heat and water for pasta in three ways: with the addition of salt in our science experiment (page 113) and starch in Spaghetti Aglio e Olio (page 116), and how to avoid a separate pot of boiling water all together in One-Pot Shells with Peas and Sausage (page 118).

NOODLE SEASON

Lots of recipes tell you to cook noodles in salty water. Does it really make a difference? Use your noodle to find out the answer in this experiment. You can use store-bought or homemade pasta sauce (see Pasta with Meat Sauce, page 82), and you can definitely eat the rest of your experiment for lunch or dinner.

TOTAL TIME: 45 minutes

LEVEL:

MATERIALS

Masking tape

Marker

2 large saucepans

2 serving bowls

Colander

2 quarts plus 2 quarts water, measured separately

8 ounces plus 8 ounces pasta, measured separately

1½ teaspoons salt

Wooden spoon

1 plate per taster

1 fork per taster

Pasta sauce (homemade or store-bought)

LET'S GO!

1 MAKE A PREDICTION Do you think pasta cooked in salty water will taste the same as pasta cooked in plain water, or do you think it will taste different? Why?

2 Make 2 masking tape labels. Use marker to write "No Salt" on 1 label and "Salt" on second label. Stick 1 label on each large saucepan (see photo, page 114).

3 Make 2 more masking tape labels. Use marker to write "No Salt" on 1 label and "Salt" on second label. Stick 1 label on each serving bowl. Set serving bowls aside.

4 Set colander in sink. Add 2 quarts water to each large saucepan. Bring water to boil over high heat.

5 Carefully add 8 ounces pasta to each saucepan of boiling water. Add 1½ teaspoons salt to saucepan labeled "Salt." Cook, stirring pasta and water in each saucepan often with wooden spoon, until pasta is tender, about 10 to 12 minutes. Turn off heat.

KEEP GOING! ⤴

Use marker and masking tape to label 1 large saucepan "No Salt" and second large saucepan "Salt."

Eat Your Experiment!

Tell tasters what the difference was between the two batches. Serve remaining sauced pasta for lunch or dinner, combining the two batches, if desired.

6 Ask an adult to drain pasta from saucepan labeled "No Salt" in colander. Transfer drained pasta from colander to serving bowl labeled "No Salt."

7 Ask an adult to drain pasta from saucepan labeled "Salt" in colander. Transfer drained pasta from colander to serving bowl labeled "Salt."

8 **OBSERVE YOUR RESULTS** Invite your family and friends to join you for a taste test—don't tell them the difference between the 2 batches of pasta until after step 9. (Turn the serving bowls so tasters can't see the labels!) Give each taster a plate and a fork. Have tasters eat a few pieces of pasta from each batch. (Ask tasters to keep their thoughts to themselves until the end of step 9.)

9 Add half of sauce to each serving bowl of pasta and use wooden spoon to stir to combine. Have tasters eat a few pieces of sauced pasta from each batch. Ask tasters:

- Did the two batches of **plain pasta taste the same or different? How so?**
- What about the **sauced pastas**—did they taste the same or different? How so?

STOP

UNDERSTANDING YOUR RESULTS
(Don't read until you've completed the experiment!)

THE BIG IDEAS

- As noodles cook, they absorb some of the hot water and go from hard and dry to tender and more flexible.
- Through diffusion (see page 11), salt moves from the salty cooking water into the noodles, seasoning them all the way through.

Pasta absorbs water and dissolved salt as it cooks, softening and seasoning the noodles.

In the Recipe Lab, all our tasters thought that the pasta cooked in salty water tasted saltier than the pasta cooked in plain water (in a good way!). Tasters also said that the pasta cooked in salty water tasted evenly seasoned. Each piece of pasta was equally salty rather than any one piece of pasta tasting very salty or not salty enough. And our tasters could detect a difference even when the pasta was coated in flavorful pesto sauce. Let's unpack this salty science!

Let's talk about salt: When you add salt to boiling water, the salt dissolves and the water itself becomes salty. As the noodles cook (see page 112), they absorb that salty water. The results? Noodles that are evenly salted, inside and out!

You might be wondering why you wouldn't just sprinkle the noodles with salt after you cook them. Great question! If you sprinkle salt on cooked noodles, they'll just taste salty on the outside—they won't be evenly seasoned throughout, because the noodles didn't absorb any salt. Plus, it's impossible to sprinkle the salt evenly over every single noodle!

One final note: Even with all that salt in their cooking water, your noodles won't taste salty like the ocean. Even though you added 1½ teaspoons of salt to the boiling water, 8 ounces of pasta only absorbs about ⅛ teaspoon of salt.

recipe

SPAGHETTI AGLIO E OLIO
(SPAGHETTI WITH GARLIC AND OIL)

SERVES: 4 to 6

TOTAL TIME: 50 minutes

LEVEL:

The water you use to cook the noodles is the starchy key to this garlicky pasta dish. Be sure to use the 3 quarts of water specified in the recipe for cooking the pasta. The starch that the pasta releases into the water is essential to achieving the proper consistency in the sauce.

PREPARE INGREDIENTS

⅓ cup extra-virgin olive oil

6–8 garlic cloves, peeled and minced (see page 16)

¼ teaspoon red pepper flakes (optional)

3 quarts water

1 pound spaghetti

1 tablespoon plus ¼ teaspoon salt, measured separately

3 tablespoons chopped fresh parsley or basil (see page 15)

GATHER COOKING EQUIPMENT

Small saucepan

Wooden spoon

Dutch oven

Ladle

4-cup liquid measuring cup

Colander

Tongs

Oven mitts

START COOKING!

1. In small saucepan, combine oil and garlic. Cook over medium-low heat, stirring often with wooden spoon, until edges of garlic are just beginning to turn golden and oil is fragrant, 5 to 7 minutes. Turn off heat and slide saucepan to cool burner.

2. Use wooden spoon to stir in pepper flakes (if using).

3. Meanwhile, add water to Dutch oven and bring water to boil over high heat. Carefully add spaghetti and 1 tablespoon salt to boiling water. Carefully use wooden spoon to push pasta down into water (ask an adult for help).

4. Cook, stirring often, until spaghetti is flexible, but still very firm in center, about 7 minutes. Turn off heat. Use ladle to carefully transfer 2½ cups cooking water to liquid measuring cup.

5. Set colander in sink. Ask an adult to carefully drain spaghetti in colander. Return drained spaghetti to now-empty Dutch oven.

6. Add oil mixture, ¼ teaspoon salt, and 2 cups reserved cooking water to Dutch oven and bring to a boil over medium-high heat. Cook, stirring often with tongs and folding pasta over itself, until water is mostly absorbed, but still pools slightly in bottom of pot, about 5 minutes (see photo, above). Turn off heat and use oven mitts to slide Dutch oven to cool burner (ask an adult for help).

7. Let pasta sit off heat for 2 minutes. Use tongs to stir in parsley or basil and additional reserved cooking water as needed (approximately ¼ cup) to adjust consistency (noodles should be slightly wet, not oily). Serve.

STIRRING AND SWIRLING

Cook, stirring often with tongs and folding pasta over itself, until water is mostly absorbed, but still pools slightly in bottom of pot, about 5 minutes.

Aglio e Olio's Secret Ingredient

Aglio e olio is a classic Italian pasta sauce made with little more than garlic and olive oil (aglio e olio means "garlic and oil" in Italian). How do these two everyday ingredients form a sauce? It's all thanks to the water you cook the pasta in. When you cook pasta, it releases starch into the boiling water. Adding that now-starchy water to the pot in step 6 means that the starch can help create a smooth sauce for the pasta. How? The pasta sauce is an emulsion (see page 123). The starch helps the oil and the pasta water come together to make a smooth—and not greasy—sauce that coats every noodle.

ONE-POT SHELLS WITH PEAS AND SAUSAGE

This pasta cooks right in the sauce (instead of separately in boiling water), so it absorbs lots of flavor—and there's fewer dishes to wash! If you can't find ground sweet Italian sausage, you can use 1 pound of sausage links; use kitchen shears to cut open the casings lengthwise and peel off and discard casings before adding to the pot in step 1.

SERVES: 2 to 4

TOTAL TIME: 1 hour

LEVEL:

PREPARE INGREDIENTS

- 1 pound ground sweet Italian sausage
- 1 small onion, peeled and chopped fine (see page 16)
- ¾ teaspoon salt
- ¼ teaspoon pepper
- ⅛–¼ teaspoon red pepper flakes (optional)
- ½ cup plus 3½ cups chicken broth, measured separately
- 4½ cups medium pasta shells (12 ounces)
- 2 cups frozen peas
- ½ cup grated Parmesan cheese (1 ounce), plus extra for serving
- 2 teaspoons grated lemon zest plus 1 tablespoon lemon juice, zested and squeezed from 1 lemon (see page 15)

GATHER COOKING EQUIPMENT

- Dutch oven with lid
- Wooden spoon
- Oven mitts
- Ladle
- Serving bowls

> **"It's the perfect recipe for dinner because the noodles were still chewy the way I like them."**
> —LOUDON, 10

START COOKING!

1. Add sausage, onion, salt, pepper, and pepper flakes (if using) to Dutch oven. Use wooden spoon to break sausage into small pieces. Cook over medium-high heat, stirring occasionally and continuing to break up sausage, until sausage is lightly browned and dark brown bits have formed on bottom of pot, 10 to 12 minutes.

2. Carefully add ½ cup chicken broth and use wooden spoon to scrape up browned bits on bottom of pot. Cook until liquid has mostly evaporated, about 2 minutes.

3. Stir in pasta and remaining 3½ cups broth. Bring mixture to boil.

4. Reduce heat to medium-low and cover pot with lid. Cook until pasta is tender, 10 to 12 minutes. (Some liquid will remain in pot.) Turn off heat.

5. Use oven mitts to remove lid. Add peas, Parmesan, lemon zest, and lemon juice. Use wooden spoon to stir vigorously for 1 minute. Let sit, uncovered, for 5 minutes to allow peas to warm through and sauce to thicken slightly. (Sauce will continue to thicken as pasta cools.)

6. Use ladle to divide pasta among individual bowls. Sprinkle with extra Parmesan cheese, if desired. Serve.

Starchy Superstar

This recipe uses just one pot to cook the pasta AND the sauce together, no draining a separate pot of boiling water required! This is possible not through magic, but through the precise measurement of the liquid needed to cook your pasta. There is JUST enough broth for the pasta to absorb and become tender, plus a little extra to create the sauce. And that sauce takes shape when you stir the pasta—hard!—after it finishes cooking. As in Spaghetti Aglio e Olio (page 116), the pasta releases starch as it cooks, helping the liquid thicken into a creamy (creamless!) sauce.

WHY DON'T oil & water MIX?

Oil and water—like cats and dogs or siblings in the back seat of a car—don't mix. Why? Water molecules are polar, which means that each one has both a positive and a negative charge, kind of like a magnet. Opposite charges attract, so the positive ends of water molecules stick to the negative ends of other water molecules, forming bonds. Oil molecules, on the other hand, are nonpolar: They don't have positive or negative charges. There's no way for them to stick to the water molecules, so they keep to themselves in their own separate layer. But sometimes we WANT oil and water to mix, like we do for a salad dressing (page 124) or a smooth sauce for pasta or vegetables (page 126). Luckily, there is a technique that gets oil and water to play nicely: mixing! Whisking or shaking together oil and water breaks the liquids into itty-bitty droplets, dispersing them evenly for the smoothest of sauces. Learn about the ingredients that will KEEP oil and water together longer in our science experiment (page 121).

SHAKE THINGS UP

Oil and water don't normally mix. But look at salad dressings: In many of them, oil and vinegar (which is made mostly of water) form a smooth, completely mixed combination—at least for a little while. What's the secret? In this experiment, you'll mix oil and vinegar on their own and then with some ingredients often found in salad dressings— will they help oil and water stay mixed?

TOTAL TIME: 1¼ hours

LEVEL:

MATERIALS

Masking tape

Marker

3 (6- to 8-ounce) clear jars with tight-fitting lids

Measuring spoons

1 cup plus 2 tablespoons extra-virgin olive oil

6 tablespoons red wine vinegar

1 teaspoon Dijon mustard

1 teaspoon mayonnaise

LET'S GO!

1 Use masking tape and marker to label 1 jar as "Control," second jar as "Mustard," and third jar as "Mayonnaise." (See page 11 to learn more about control samples in experiments.)

2 Add 6 tablespoons oil to each jar. Add 2 tablespoons vinegar to each jar. Screw lid tightly on jar labeled "Control."

3 Add mustard to jar labeled "Mustard." Screw lid tightly on jar.

4 Add mayonnaise to jar labeled "Mayonnaise." Screw lid tightly on jar.

KEEP GOING! ↷

VINAIGRETTE DANCE PARTY

If you've got a friend or sibling handy, one of you can shake two jars and the other can shake the remaining jar. Turn on some tunes and have a 30-second dance party!

Eat Your Experiment!

Turn your emulsions into a salad dressing. Add contents of 1 or more jars to large airtight container with lid. For each jar you use, add ¼ teaspoon **salt** and ⅛ teaspoon **pepper** to container. Place lid on container and shake to combine ingredients. Dressing can be refrigerated for up to 1 week. Shake well before using.

5 Hold 1 jar in each hand. Vigorously shake jars for 30 seconds (see photo, page 122). Set aside jars. Repeat shaking with remaining jar.

6 MAKE A PREDICTION In which jar do you predict that the oil and vinegar will stay mixed the longest: the control jar, the mustard jar, or the mayonnaise jar? Why do you think so?

7 OBSERVE YOUR RESULTS What do the jars look like right after you finish shaking them? Check on your jars every 15 minutes until 45 minutes have passed. What do you notice? Which jar kept the oil and vinegar mixed the longest? The shortest?

STOP UNDERSTANDING YOUR RESULTS
(Don't read until you've completed the experiment!)

THE BIG IDEAS

- A mixture of oil and water—called an emulsion—quickly separates back into two separate layers once you stop shaking or mixing it.
- Special molecules called emulsifiers bridge the gap between oil and vinegar, keeping the emulsion smooth and combined for much longer.
- Mayonnaise and mustard are two ingredients that contain emulsifiers.

CONTROL MAYONNAISE MUSTARD

0 Minutes

CONTROL MAYONNAISE MUSTARD

15 Minutes

CONTROL MAYONNAISE MUSTARD

30 Minutes

In the Recipe Lab, we found that the mixture in the mayonnaise jar stayed mixed the longest. The mixture in the mustard jar came in a close second, and the mixture in the control jar separated back into two layers after less than 15 minutes. How long did the mixtures in your jars stay combined?

When you shake or whisk oil and vinegar (which is mostly water), the two liquids form what's called an emulsion ("ih-MUHL-shun"). "Emulsion" is a scientific word for a combination of two liquids that don't usually mix. But this emulsion won't last long—the oil and vinegar retreat into two separate layers after just a few minutes. (An emulsion of oil and vinegar is called a vinaigrette, and it's often used as a salad dressing or sauce.)

To get oil and water to STAY mixed, you need some help from an emulsifier. Emulsifiers are special molecules that bridge the gap between two liquids that don't want to get along, such as oil and water. One end of an emulsifier molecule is attracted to water. The other end is attracted to oil (imagine that the emulsifier is holding hands with oil on one side and water on the other). Mustard and mayonnaise both contain emulsifiers, so a vinaigrette made with mustard or mayonnaise will stay combined for much longer than one made with just oil and vinegar. So which one should you use when making a vinaigrette? You pick—whichever you like best!

CONTROL MAYONNAISE MUSTARD

45 Minutes

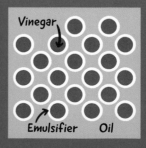

Vinegar

Emulsifier   Oil

recipe

MISO-HONEY VINAIGRETTE WITH SALAD

SERVES: 4

TOTAL TIME: 25 minutes

LEVEL:

This "shake-ahead" salad dressing harnesses the power of mayonnaise and two different oils to stay emulsified and pourable straight from the refrigerator. If you can't find Persian cucumbers, use half of an English cucumber instead.

PREPARE INGREDIENTS

DRESSING

2 tablespoons white miso

1 tablespoon mayonnaise

2 teaspoons honey

¼ cup unseasoned rice vinegar

¼ teaspoon salt

¼ cup plus ¼ cup extra-virgin olive oil, measured separately

¼ cup vegetable oil

SALAD

4 cups mixed baby lettuce (4 ounces)

2 Persian cucumbers, ends trimmed and chopped

1 cup snow peas, strings removed and cut in half (see page 127)

1 tablespoon toasted sesame seeds (optional, see page 125)

GATHER COOKING EQUIPMENT

1 (12- to 16-ounce) jar with tight-fitting lid

Fork

Large bowl

Liquid measuring cup

Tongs

To toast sesame seeds, add sesame seeds to 8-inch or 10-inch skillet. Toast over medium-low heat, stirring often with rubber spatula, until seeds turn golden brown, 3 to 5 minutes. Turn off heat. Transfer seeds to small bowl and let cool completely, about 10 minutes.

START COOKING!

1. FOR THE DRESSING Add miso, mayonnaise, and honey to jar. Use fork to stir until mixture is well combined.

2. Add vinegar and salt and cover jar with lid to seal. Shake until smooth, about 10 seconds.

3. Remove lid. Add ¼ cup olive oil and re-cover jar with lid. Shake until combined, about 10 seconds. Add remaining ¼ cup olive oil and repeat shaking.

4. Add vegetable oil and shake until dressing is smooth and slightly thickened. (Dressing can be refrigerated for up to 1 week. Shake briefly before using.)

5. FOR THE SALAD In large bowl, combine lettuce, cucumbers, and snow peas. Measure out ¼ cup dressing and drizzle over salad. Use tongs to toss until salad is well coated with dressing. Sprinkle salad with sesame seeds (if using). Serve.

Perfectly Pourable!

We didn't want to create a salad dressing that would stay emulsified for just a few minutes. We wanted a salad dressing that would stay emulsified for so long that you could pour it straight from the refrigerator! To do this, we first used a superstrong emulsifier: mayonnaise. And then we added some vegetable oil. Vinaigrettes are traditionally made with just olive oil, but when olive oil is kept in the refrigerator, its molecules harden into a solid mass that is impossible to pour. Adding vegetable oil to the mixture prevents the olive oil from crystallizing. Success!

BUTTERY SUGAR SNAP PEAS

SERVES: 4

TOTAL TIME: 45 minutes

LEVEL:

Dress up sugar snap peas with a buttery sauce that's smooth and velvety thanks to the power of emulsions. If your sugar snap peas are labeled "stringless," you can skip step 1.

PREPARE INGREDIENTS

- 1 pound sugar snap peas
- 1 cup water
- 1 tablespoon finely chopped shallot (see page 16)
- ¾ teaspoon white wine vinegar
- ¼ teaspoon salt
  Pinch sugar
- 2 tablespoons unsalted butter, cut into 2 pieces and chilled

GATHER COOKING EQUIPMENT

Large saucepan with lid

Steamer basket

Oven mitts

Large plate

Liquid measuring cup

1-tablespoon measuring spoon

Whisk

Wooden spoon

START COOKING!

1. Working with 1 snap pea at a time, snap off tip and grasp string (see photo, below). Pull string along flat side of snap pea to remove it.

2. In large saucepan, bring water to boil over high heat. Place snap peas in steamer basket. Use oven mitts to carefully lower basket into saucepan (ask an adult for help).

3. Cover saucepan with lid. Cook snap peas for 2 minutes. Turn off heat.

4. Use oven mitts to remove lid and lift steamer basket out of saucepan (ask an adult for help). Place steamer basket on large plate.

5. Slide saucepan to cool burner and let cool slightly, about 3 minutes. Hold saucepan handle with oven mitts and carefully pour water from saucepan into liquid measuring cup (ask an adult for help).

6. Measure out 2 tablespoons water from liquid measuring cup and transfer back to large saucepan.

7. Add shallot, vinegar, salt, and sugar to saucepan. Whisk until sugar and salt are dissolved. Cook over medium heat until mixture is bubbling, 1 to 2 minutes.

8. Reduce heat to low. Add 1 piece butter to saucepan. Whisk constantly until butter is melted and incorporated, about 45 seconds. Repeat with second piece butter, whisking until sauce is thick and smooth, about 1 minute.

9. Carefully add snap peas back to saucepan and use wooden spoon to stir until coated with sauce. Cook until snap peas are warmed through, 1 to 2 minutes. Turn off heat. Serve.

Don't Cry, Emulsify!

The key to this velvety sauce is not just butter—it's cold butter added slowly to the pan. What?!

No surprise, but this sauce is an emulsion (see page 123). It's made from water and butter, which normally don't like to mix—that's why we whisk the sauce constantly as we make it. But butter itself is a mixture of fat and water, too. If all the butter were added to the pan at once, allowing it to melt unchecked, it would separate into greasy fat and water. But slowly adding the cold butter into the hot water—with constant whisking—breaks up the tiny fat droplets as they melt, turning the sauce into a creamy and thick emulsion.

HOW TO PREP SNAP PEAS

Working with 1 snap pea at a time, snap off tip and grasp string. Pull string along flat side of snap pea to remove it.

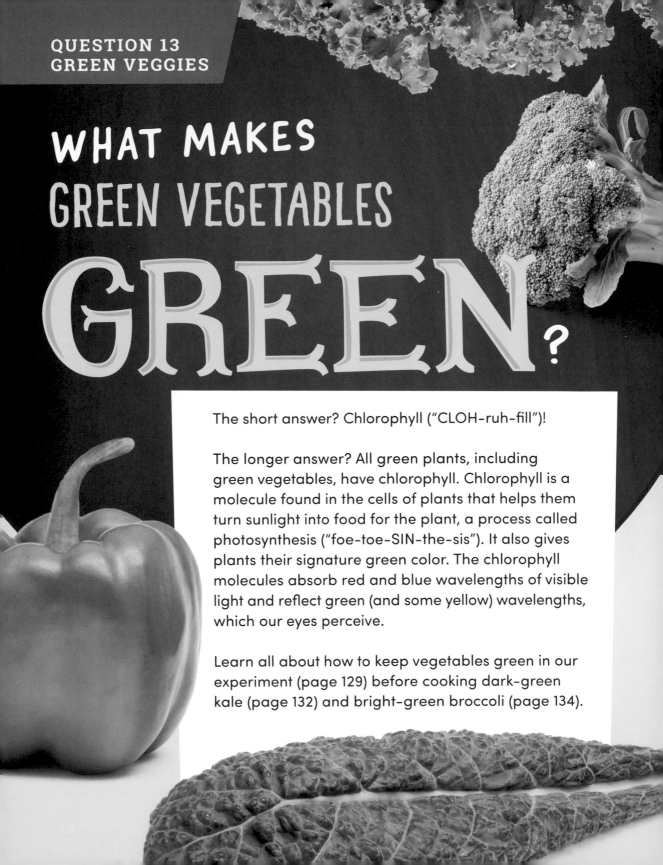

WHAT MAKES GREEN VEGETABLES GREEN?

The short answer? Chlorophyll ("CLOH-ruh-fill")!

The longer answer? All green plants, including green vegetables, have chlorophyll. Chlorophyll is a molecule found in the cells of plants that helps them turn sunlight into food for the plant, a process called photosynthesis ("foe-toe-SIN-the-sis"). It also gives plants their signature green color. The chlorophyll molecules absorb red and blue wavelengths of visible light and reflect green (and some yellow) wavelengths, which our eyes perceive.

Learn all about how to keep vegetables green in our experiment (page 129) before cooking dark-green kale (page 132) and bright-green broccoli (page 134).

IT'S EASY BEING GREEN

Learn some of the secrets to keeping green vegetables bright green when you cook them—and make yourself a veggie side dish—in this steamy experiment.

TOTAL TIME: 40 minutes

LEVEL:

MATERIALS

- Masking tape
- Marker
- Serving platter
- 10-inch skillet with lid
- ¼ cup plus ¼ cup water, measured separately
- 1½ cups (4 ounces) plus 1½ cups (4 ounces) broccoli florets, measured separately, large florets cut in half
- Wooden spoon
- Oven mitts
- 1 tablespoon lemon juice, squeezed from ½ lemon
- 1 small plate per taster
- 1 fork per taster

LET'S GO!

1 MAKE A PREDICTION Which do you think will turn out greener after it's cooked: broccoli cooked plain or broccoli cooked with lemon juice? Why do you think so?

2 Use masking tape and marker to label 1 side of serving platter "Water" and opposite side of serving platter "Water + Lemon Juice."

3 In 10-inch skillet, bring ¼ cup water to boil over medium-high heat. Add 1½ cups broccoli to skillet. Use wooden spoon to gently toss until combined.

4 Cover skillet and reduce heat to medium-low (see photo, page 130). Cook broccoli for 2 minutes.

5 Use oven mitts to carefully remove lid from skillet. Use wooden spoon to gently toss broccoli. Cover skillet and continue to cook until broccoli is crisp-tender, 2 to 4 minutes longer. Turn off heat and slide skillet to cool burner.

KEEP GOING!

COVER THE SKILLET

Covering the skillet traps the hot steam inside, which helps to quickly cook the broccoli.

Eat Your Experiment!

Enjoy one or both batches of broccoli as a side dish. Add broccoli to now-empty skillet. Cook over low heat until broccoli is warmed through, 1 to 2 minutes. If desired, toss broccoli with 1 tablespoon **extra-virgin olive oil** or 1 tablespoon **melted butter**, ⅛ teaspoon **salt**, and sprinkle with 1 tablespoon **grated Parmesan cheese**.

6 Use oven mitts to carefully remove lid. Transfer broccoli to "Water" side of serving platter (ask an adult for help).

7 Add remaining ¼ cup water to skillet and bring to boil over medium-high heat. Add lemon juice and remaining broccoli to skillet. Use wooden spoon to gently toss until combined.

8 Cook broccoli, following steps 4 through 6, above. Transfer broccoli to "Water + Lemon Juice" side of serving platter (ask an adult for help).

9 **OBSERVE YOUR RESULTS** Look at the 2 batches of broccoli—what do you notice about the broccoli's color? Which batch is greener? Take a taste of each batch. Which do you prefer?

STOP

UNDERSTANDING YOUR RESULTS
(Don't read until you've completed the experiment!)

THE BIG IDEAS

- Adding acid, such as lemon juice or vinegar, to green vegetables causes them to turn a yellow-gray color.
- The acid changes the structure of the bright green chlorophyll molecules in the vegetable's plant cells, creating new yellow or gray-green molecules.

No Lemon Juice
Broccoli Stays Bright Green

Lemon Juice
Broccoli Turns Yellow-Gray

In the Recipe Lab, the broccoli we steamed with plain water turned bright green while the broccoli cooked with lemon juice turned yellow-gray anywhere the lemon juice touched the broccoli florets. How did your broccoli turn out?

As green vegetables start to cook, tiny air pockets between the vegetable's plant cells expand and gas trapped inside is released. With that air out of the way, we're able to see the vegetable's bright green chlorophyll even more clearly. That's why the broccoli steamed with just water was even brighter green than raw broccoli.

But just as kryptonite weakens Superman, acids are the enemy of chlorophyll. When a green vegetable comes in contact with an acid, the acid changes the structure of the chlorophyll molecules in the vegetable's plant cells. They transform from bright green chlorophyll into two new molecules: gray-green pheophytin a ("fee-oh-FYE-tin") and yellow pheophytin b.

If you're cooking a green vegetable and want to add an acidic ingredient, such as lemon juice, lime juice, or vinegar, don't add it until the very end (see Garlicky Kale, page 132). That gives the acid less time to react with the chlorophyll molecules. Plus, if you've cooked the vegetable with oil, the oil will form a protective barrier around the vegetable. One final tip: You can add lemon or lime flavor without adding acidic lemon or lime juice—just add the (non-acidic) zest instead (see Pan-Steamed Broccoli, page 134).

recipe

GARLICKY KALE

Cooking kale quickly with a liquid is the key to turning its tough leaves tender—AND keeping their deep-green color. We prefer using curly kale that you stem yourself. You can substitute prechopped bagged curly kale, but the stems will be chewy.

SERVES: 4

TOTAL TIME: 30 minutes

LEVEL:

PREPARE INGREDIENTS

- 1 pound curly kale
- 1 cup chicken or vegetable broth
- 2 tablespoons plus 1 tablespoon extra-virgin olive oil, measured separately
- 2 garlic cloves, peeled and minced (see page 16)
- ¼ teaspoon salt
- ⅛ teaspoon red pepper flakes
- 1 teaspoon lemon juice, squeezed from ½ lemon

GATHER COOKING EQUIPMENT

Dutch oven with lid

Oven mitts

Wooden spoon

Small bowl

There are several varieties of kale. Curly kale is lighter green, Lacinato kale is darker green, and red kale's stems are a deep purple. How do they get their different colors? Plants get their green color from chlorophyll (see page 128). But there are two types of chlorophyll: chlorophyll a, which is bright blue-green in color, and chlorophyll b, which is olive green. Plants that grow in areas with more intense sunlight need less chlorophyll to convert sunlight into energy. They tend to be lighter in color and contain more chlorophyll a—like curly kale. Plants that grow in shaded areas have more chlorophyll overall, to make the most of the sunlight they get. They also have more chlorophyll b, making them darker in color—like Lacinato!

START COOKING!

1. Use your hands to separate stems of kale from leaves following photo below; discard stems. Tear leaves into 2-inch pieces.

2. In Dutch oven, bring broth and 2 tablespoons oil to boil over high heat. Carefully add kale to pot. Cover pot and reduce heat to medium-high. Cook kale for 3 minutes.

3. Use oven mitts to carefully remove lid from Dutch oven. Use wooden spoon to stir kale. Use oven mitts to cover pot and cook until kale is tender, about 4 minutes.

4. While kale cooks, in small bowl combine garlic, salt, pepper flakes, and remaining 1 tablespoon oil.

5. Use oven mitts to carefully remove lid from Dutch oven. Increase heat to high and cook, stirring often, until remaining liquid has evaporated and kale starts to sizzle, 1 to 2 minutes. Turn off heat.

6. Use wooden spoon to push kale to 1 side of pot. Add garlic mixture to now-empty side of pot and cook until garlic is fragrant, about 1 minute.

7. Add lemon juice and toss kale with garlic mixture until evenly coated. Serve.

HOW TO STEM KALE

Hold end of kale stem in one hand. Pinch thumb and index finger of your other hand on either side of stem. Slide your hand down length of stem from bottom to top to strip leaf from stem. Discard stem.

PAN-STEAMED BROCCOLI WITH LEMON

A steamy skillet cooks broccoli quickly—helping it keep its color a vibrant green.

SERVES: 4

TOTAL TIME: 25 minutes

LEVEL:

PREPARE INGREDIENTS

- ⅓ cup water
- 1 pound (6 cups) broccoli florets, large florets cut in half
- ½ teaspoon salt
- 2 tablespoons unsalted butter, cut into 4 pieces
- ½ teaspoon grated lemon zest, zested from ½ lemon
- ¼ teaspoon pepper

GATHER COOKING EQUIPMENT

- 12-inch skillet with lid
- Oven mitts
- Wooden spoon

> **"It was so good! I don't like broccoli too and I got several servings!"**
> —KENDALL, 10

START COOKING!

1. In 12-inch skillet, bring water to boil over high heat. Add broccoli to skillet and sprinkle with salt. Cover skillet and reduce heat to medium-low. Cook broccoli for 4 minutes.

2. Use oven mitts to carefully remove lid from skillet. Use wooden spoon to gently toss broccoli. Cover skillet and cook until broccoli is bright green and crisp-tender, 3 to 5 minutes.

3. Use oven mitts to carefully remove lid. Cook until remaining liquid evaporates, about 1 minute. Turn off heat and slide skillet to cool burner.

4. Use wooden spoon to push broccoli to 1 side of skillet. Add butter, lemon zest, and pepper to now-empty side of skillet and stir until butter melts.

5. Toss broccoli with butter mixture until evenly coated. Serve.

Bright-Green Broccoli

As we now know, green vegetables get their color from chlorophyll. Plants store chlorophyll inside their cells in tiny containers called chloroplasts. In raw vegetables, there are lots of microscopic air pockets in between plant cells (think of them kind of like bubble wrap). Those air pockets deflect light, making raw vegetables look duller green than they actually are. When we cook broccoli and other green vegetables, those tiny air pockets expand, the air in them escapes, and the air pockets collapse like popped balloons. All of a sudden, we can see the vegetable's true bright-green color! That's why broccoli looks brighter green when it starts cooking than it does raw. Beware: The structure of chlorophyll is fragile and that bright-green color is fleeting. The longer green vegetables are cooked, the more chlorophyll breaks down, turning them from bright green to drab. And we know that acids are chlorophyll's archnemesis. Here we use lemon zest to add lemon flavor without any acidic lemon juice.

WHAT'S THE DIFFERENCE BETWEEN BROWN & WHITE RICE?

There are thousands of different types of rice grown around the world. But most have one thing in common: They can be either brown or white, depending on how they're processed.

Every type of rice is covered with a protective husk when it's harvested. Remove the husk, and you have brown rice! Remove three more layers of each rice grain—called the bran, germ, and aleurone layers—and you're left with white rice. Because brown rice contains the fiber-rich bran and fatty germ, it contains more nutrients—and more flavor.

Do white rice and brown rice cook differently? Does one take longer than the other? Discover that (and more!) in our science experiment (page 137). And then cook some deliciously starchy risotto (page 140) made of white Arborio rice and colorful Rainbow Grain Bowls (page 142) that feature a brown rice base.

RICE TO MEET YOU

You'll find white rice and brown rice on the shelf of nearly every grocery store. Other than color, what makes them different? Find out—and make two batches of fluffy rice to eat—in this experiment. You can use long-grain white and brown rice instead of short-grain, if you prefer.

TOTAL TIME: 45 minutes

LEVEL:

MATERIALS

1 quart plus 1 quart water, measured separately

2 large saucepans

1 cup short-grain white rice

Fine-mesh strainer

4 bowls (2 medium, 2 small)

1 cup short-grain brown rice

¼ teaspoon plus ¼ teaspoon salt, measured separately

Wooden spoon

Colander

1 plate per taster

1 fork per taster

LET'S GO!

1 MAKE A PREDICTION Do you think white rice and brown rice will take the same amount of time to cook? Do you think they will have the same flavor and texture after they're cooked, or will they be different? Why do you think so?

_____

2 Add 1 quart water to each large saucepan. Bring water to boil over high heat.

_____

3 Place white rice in fine-mesh strainer and rinse under cold running water (see photo, page 138). Stir white rice occasionally with your fingers until water runs clear, about 1 minute. Transfer drained white rice to 1 medium bowl. Repeat rinsing and draining with brown rice.

_____

4 Carefully add drained brown rice and ¼ teaspoon salt to 1 saucepan. Add drained white rice and remaining ¼ teaspoon salt to second saucepan.

KEEP GOING! ↵

Eat Your Experiment!

Use your cooked rice as the base for **Rainbow Grain Bowls** (page 142), serve it alongside **Chana Masala** (page 100), or toss it with **melted butter** and a sprinkle of **salt** for a simple side dish.

RINSING WHITE RICE

Rinsing white rice removes excess starch from its surface.

5 Set timer for 5 minutes. Reduce heat to medium and simmer (small bubbles should break often across surface of water), stirring rice in both saucepans occasionally with wooden spoon.

6 After 5 minutes, use wooden spoon to remove a few grains of white rice from saucepan. Place in 1 small bowl. Repeat with brown rice and second small bowl. Set timer again for 5 minutes. Let grains of rice cool slightly.

7 Taste cooled grains of each type of rice: If grains are hard, rice is not ready and needs more time to cook. If grains are tender (easy to bite through) and slightly chewy, rice is ready. Discard remaining rice in small bowls.

8 Continue tasting a few grains of each batch of rice every 5 minutes until rice is tender. (One type of rice might take longer to cook than the other!)

9 When 1 batch of rice is tender, place colander in sink. Turn off heat. Carefully pour rice into colander (ask an adult for help). Transfer drained rice to 1 medium bowl. Return colander to sink.

10 When second batch of rice is tender, turn off heat. Carefully pour rice into colander (ask an adult for help). Transfer drained rice to second medium bowl.

11 **OBSERVE YOUR RESULTS** Which batch of rice took longer to cook, the white rice or the brown rice? Invite your friends and family to join you for a taste test. Give each taster a fork and a small spoonful of white and brown rice on a plate. How would they describe the flavor and texture of each type of rice? How are they similar? How are they different?

STOP UNDERSTANDING YOUR RESULTS
(Don't read until you've completed the experiment!)

THE BIG IDEAS

- White rice is brown rice that has had the bran, germ, and aleurone layers removed.
- Rice absorbs hot water as it cooks, which makes the grains softer and more tender.
- The bran layer of brown rice causes it to absorb water more slowly and take longer to cook.

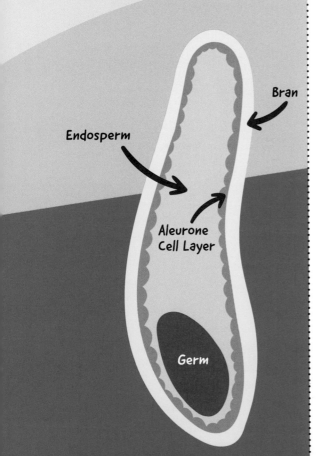

Endosperm

Bran

Aleurone
Cell Layer

Germ

In the Recipe Lab, we observed that the white rice cooked much faster than the brown rice. What did you observe?

All rice is the seed of a plant. When rice is harvested, it's covered with a protective husk. Once that husk is removed, you've got a grain of brown rice. Grains of brown rice have several layers: The outer, protective layer is called the bran (it's full of nutritious fiber). Underneath the bran, you'll discover the thin aleurone layer, which is full of enzymes and surrounds the germ and the endosperm. The germ is what would eventually grow into a new rice plant (remember, rice is a seed!). The endosperm is full of starch, which would provide food for the growing rice plant.

Manufacturers mill brown rice to remove the bran and the germ, and then they polish it to remove the aleurone layer. Just the endosperm is left behind, which is also called . . . white rice. That's right! White rice is simply brown rice with a few layers removed.

Like pasta (see page 112), grains of rice start out hard and dry. As they cook in boiling water, the grains absorb some of that water and become softer and more flexible. Because brown rice still contains the bran, it absorbs water much more slowly than white rice does. That's why brown rice takes so much longer to cook.

As you rinsed the white rice, some of the starch on the surface of the rice came off—that's what made the water cloudy. Since brown rice's starchy endosperm is covered by its bran, its starch stayed trapped inside and the water stayed clear. Recipes typically call for rinsing white rice because that surface starch can make the cooked rice sticky.

RISOTTO WITH PARMESAN AND HERBS

This Italian rice dish is ultracreamy but contains no cream! The secrets to its texture? Using a special type of rice and some extra stirring. You can use Carnaroli rice instead of Arborio rice in this recipe.

SERVES: 4

TOTAL TIME: 1 hour

LEVEL:

PREPARE INGREDIENTS

- 3 cups chicken broth
- 1 cup water
- 2 tablespoons unsalted butter
- 1 small onion, peeled and chopped fine (see page 16)
- ½ teaspoon salt
- 1 garlic clove, peeled and minced (see page 16)
- 1 cup Arborio rice
- ½ cup grated Parmesan cheese (1 ounce)
- 2 tablespoons chopped fresh parsley or chives (optional)
- 1 tablespoon lemon juice, squeezed from ½ lemon

GATHER COOKING EQUIPMENT

Small saucepan with lid

Ladle

Liquid measuring cup

Small plate

Large saucepan with lid

Wooden spoon

Oven mitts

START COOKING!

1. In small saucepan, combine chicken broth and water. Bring to simmer over medium-high heat (small bubbles should break often across surface of mixture). Turn off heat.

2. Use ladle to carefully measure 1 cup broth mixture into liquid measuring cup. Cover with small plate and set aside. Cover small saucepan with lid to keep warm.

3. In large saucepan, melt butter over medium heat. Add onion and salt. Cook, stirring often with wooden spoon, until onion is softened, about 5 minutes.

4. Stir in garlic and cook for 30 seconds. Add rice and cook, stirring often, for 2 minutes.

5. Use oven mitts to remove lid from small saucepan. Carefully pour all of broth mixture from small saucepan into rice mixture (ask an adult for help—saucepan will be hot and mixture will bubble and steam). Use wooden spoon to stir to combine.

6. Reduce heat to medium-low, cover large saucepan with lid, and cook for 5 minutes.

7. Use oven mitts to remove lid from large saucepan and stir. Replace lid and cook until almost all liquid is absorbed and rice is tender but still chewy, 12 to 14 minutes, repeating stirring halfway through cooking.

8. Use oven mitts to remove lid. Remove plate from liquid measuring cup and stir in half of reserved broth mixture. Stir rice gently and constantly until risotto becomes creamy, 2 to 3 minutes (see photo, right). Turn off heat. Stir in Parmesan cheese. Cover pot with lid and let sit for 5 minutes.

9. Use oven mitts to remove lid. Stir in parsley (if using) and lemon juice. If needed, stir in remaining broth mixture, a little bit at a time, until risotto is loosened slightly. Serve immediately.

Getting to Know Arborio

There's something very special about risotto and its combination of tender—but not mushy—grains of rice surrounded by a creamy sauce. Arborio ("are-BORE-ee-oh") rice is responsible for much of risotto's iconic texture. Short-grain Arborio rice is ideal for risotto because it contains lots of starch. It's usually sold as white rice, which means there is no protective bran layer present to keep all that starch inside. So, as the rice cooks, it releases starch granules, which absorb the liquid broth and expand, giving the risotto its rich consistency. What's more, the unique starch at the very center of grains of Arborio rice doesn't soften and break down very easily—it gives the rice a firm, al dente center, even once the outside of the rice is tender.

WHEN THE RICE BECOMES CREAMY

Stir rice gently and constantly until risotto becomes creamy, 2 to 3 minutes. As the rice cooks in the liquid broth mixture, starch from the rice absorbs the liquid, giving it a thicker, creamy consistency.

SERVES: 4

TOTAL TIME: 1 hour and 10 minutes

LEVEL:

recipe

RAINBOW GRAIN BOWLS

Cooking brown rice like pasta is one way to make sure that you get perfectly tender rice, every time! While the rice cooks, prepare the remaining parts of the recipe.

PREPARE INGREDIENTS

- 1 cup unseasoned rice vinegar
- 3 tablespoons sugar
- ½ teaspoon plus 1 teaspoon salt, measured separately
- 2 cups shredded red cabbage
- 6 cups water
- 1¾ cups short-grain brown rice
- 1 (15-ounce) can chickpeas or white beans, opened
- ½ teaspoon ground turmeric
- 1 tablespoon plus ¼ cup extra-virgin olive oil, measured separately
- 2 tablespoons lime juice, squeezed from 1 lime
- 2 teaspoons low-sodium soy sauce
- 1 teaspoon honey
- ¼ teaspoon ground ginger
- 1½ cups (9 ounces) cherry tomatoes, cut in half
- 2 carrots, peeled into ribbons (see page 143)
- 1 avocado, halved, pitted, and chopped (see page 177)

GATHER COOKING EQUIPMENT

- 4 bowls (1 large, 1 medium, 2 medium microwave-safe)
- Oven mitts
- Spoon
- Large saucepan
- Wooden spoon
- Colander
- Whisk
- 4 serving bowls

START COOKING!

1. In 1 medium microwave-safe bowl, combine vinegar, sugar, and ½ teaspoon salt. Heat in microwave until beginning to bubble at edges, 1 to 2 minutes.

2. Use oven mitts to remove bowl from microwave. Stir mixture with spoon until sugar dissolves. Add cabbage to bowl and stir to combine. Let sit, stirring occasionally, for 45 minutes.

3. In large saucepan, bring water to boil over high heat. Carefully add rice and remaining 1 teaspoon salt to saucepan. Reduce heat to medium and simmer, stirring occasionally with wooden spoon, until rice is tender, 30 to 35 minutes.

4. While rice cooks, set colander in sink. Pour chickpeas into colander. Rinse chickpeas with cold water and shake colander to drain well. Transfer chickpeas to second medium microwave-safe bowl. Rinse colander and leave in sink.

5. Add turmeric and 1 tablespoon oil to chickpeas and use spoon to stir until evenly coated. Heat in microwave until warmed through, about 1 minute. Use oven mitts to remove bowl from microwave; set aside.

6. In medium bowl, whisk together lime juice, soy sauce, honey, and ginger. While whisking constantly, slowly pour in remaining ¼ cup oil until combined.

7. When rice is tender, carefully pour into now-empty colander in sink (ask an adult for help). Carefully shake colander to drain well. Transfer drained rice to large bowl. Pour half of lime dressing over rice. Use wooden spoon to stir until rice is evenly coated.

8. Divide rice evenly among 4 serving bowls. Top each bowl with piles of tomatoes, carrot ribbons, chickpeas, avocado, and pickled cabbage, placing piles around bowl in rainbow order. Use spoon to drizzle each bowl with remaining dressing. Serve.

HOW TO MAKE CARROT RIBBONS

Peel carrots, then trim off ends. Use vegetable peeler to peel off 3 ribbons from 1 side of carrot (peeling away from you). Turn carrot and peel off 3 more ribbons. Continue to turn and peel ribbons from rest of first carrot. Repeat with remaining carrot.

Don't Toil, Boil!

Many recipes call for cooking rice in a measured amount of water until all the water is absorbed and the rice is tender. But you can also treat it like pasta: Cook the brown rice in a big pot of water until it's tender, then drain it in a colander. As the rice cooks in the boiling water, the grains move around and absorb hot water from all sides, which helps the rice cook evenly. Plus, cooking brown rice using the pasta method is much faster than waiting for all the water to absorb.

ARE Beans A VEGETABLE?

As the saying goes: "Beans, beans, the magical fruit . . ." and you know the rest. But are beans actually a fruit!? Technically, they are! More specifically, they are the seeds of fruits. They come from the legume family, a family of plants that produce edible seeds inside protective pods. Today we're talking about a particular member of the legume family, a type of bean that is grown and harvested to be dried. They're called pulses ("PUHL-ses"). Lentils, chickpeas, and navy beans are all examples of pulses. They are dried in their pods until they're hard, which allows them to stay on your shelf for a long time. Explore how they grow in a hands-on activity (page 145). And then learn how to turn the dried seeds into creamy Simple White Beans with Garlic (page 148). Finally, work with canned black beans to make vegetarian Black Bean Burgers (page 150).

BEAN THERE, DONE THAT

Grow a new bean plant . . . from a bean! You can substitute dried pinto beans, black beans, chickpeas, or lentils for the dried cannellini or kidney beans, but they might take a different amount of time to sprout. Do not eat these bean sprouts—warm, moist zipper-lock bags are a good place to grow beans, but they're also a good place to grow harmful bacteria. These beans are for learning only!

TOTAL TIME: 10 minutes, plus 1 to 2 weeks soaking and sprouting time

LEVEL: ▲

LET'S GO!

1 Place beans in small jar. Cover with water by 1 inch. Place lid on jar. Let beans soak for 8 hours or overnight.

2 Lightly wet paper towel with water and gently squeeze to remove excess water. Fold paper towel and slide it into zipper-lock bag so it lies flat.

3 Remove soaked beans from jar; discard water. Place beans in zipper-lock bag, about 1 inch apart. Seal bag, leaving 1- to 2-inch opening to allow airflow.

4 Use masking tape to attach zipper-lock bag to window with beans facing out following photo, page 146.

MATERIALS

5 dried cannellini or kidney beans

Small jar with lid

Paper towel

Water

Zipper-lock bag

Masking tape

Paper

Pencil and/or marker

Ruler

Small containers for planting, such as clean, empty yogurt containers (optional)

Potting soil (optional)

KEEP GOING! ↷

IT'S A BEANBAG!

Attach your zipper-lock bag to a window with the beans facing out. (Look for a window that gets indirect sunlight—you don't want to scorch your beans! If it's very cold where you live, tape the bag to a shelf or wall near a window. If the beans are too cold, they won't grow.)

ABOUT THAT SPROUT

Plant the sprouted beans with the white roots facing down into the soil and the green shoots facing up toward the sun.

5 MAKE A PREDICTION What do you think will happen to the beans as they sit in the bag for the next few days?

6 OBSERVE YOUR RESULTS Every day, observe your beans up close. What do you notice? How are they changing? Record and draw your observations on a sheet of paper. Use a ruler to measure any growth each day. (If paper towel appears dried out, lightly spray inside of zipper-lock bag with water. Reseal bag, leaving 1- to 2-inch opening for airflow.)

7 Continue observing and measuring your beans and recording your observations for at least 5 to 7 days, or until beans have sprouted.

8 You can plant your sprouted beans in soil and watch them continue to grow! Fill 1 small container for each sprouted bean about ¾ of the way with potting soil. Use your finger to make small hole in soil, about 1 inch deep. Place 1 spouted bean in hole with root end (white growth) facing down into soil and shoot (green growth) facing upward (see photo, left). Cover bean loosely with soil, leaving shoot exposed. Repeat with remaining sprouted beans, if desired.

9 Place containers in sunny location, such as a windowsill. Every day, add about 1 tablespoon water to each container (soil should be wet but not soggy). Continue to observe, measure, and record your beans' growth over time. How would you describe the plants? Short? Tall? Delicate? Leafy? Sturdy?

STOP UNDERSTANDING YOUR RESULTS
(Don't read until you've completed the activity!)

THE BIG IDEAS

- Beans are the seeds of legume plants—under the right conditions, they can grow into new plants.
- Beans are made of four main parts: the seed coat, the embryo, the cotyledons, and the hilum.

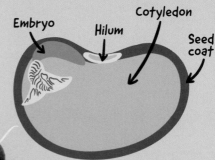

Here in the Recipe Lab, our pinto beans had ½-inch to 1-inch sprouts after just 5 days. When we planted our sprouts in soil, they really took off! We had 5-inch-tall bean plants just 1 week after we planted them. How did your sprouts grow?

Beans are the seeds of legume plants. In nature, when the legume plant's pods are fully grown, they become dry and delicate. When they're jostled, say by the wind or a passing animal, the pods can easily open, letting the beans fall to the ground where, if the conditions are right, they can start growing into new legume plants.

A single bean has four main parts. The thin seed coat surrounds and protects the inside of the bean. The embryo will eventually grow into a new legume plant. The two cotyledons provide nutrients for the embryo in the forms of starch and

proteins (and make up the bulk of the bean). The hilum—the little dent in the bean—is where the bean was once attached to its pod and where the bean absorbs water during soaking, in the zipper-lock bag, and in the soil.

When our pinto and kidney beans sprouted, a small white sprout was the first thing to emerge from the bean—this is the main root of the bean plant. A little later, another sprout surfaced—one that was green and curved. This will become the main stem of the bean plant. Once we planted our sprouts in soil, the stems straightened out and we also observed the bean's two cotyledons split apart. Around this time, our plant grew its first little leaves! Eventually, the cotyledons fell off of the plant and even more leaves started to grow.

recipe

SIMPLE WHITE BEANS WITH GARLIC

SERVES: 4 to 6

TOTAL TIME: 1½ hours, plus 8 to 24 hours brining time

LEVEL:

Dried cannellini beans cook up perfectly tender thanks to a salty soak. Plan ahead! The beans need to soak for at least 8 hours before cooking. If you can't find dried cannellini beans, you can use dried Great Northern beans instead and increase the cooking time in step 6 to 40 to 45 minutes. Serve as a side dish with chicken or pork, or as a topping for a salad or grain bowl.

PREPARE INGREDIENTS

- 4 cups plus 5 cups water, measured separately
- 2¼ teaspoons plus 1½ teaspoons salt, measured separately
- 8 ounces dried cannellini beans
- ¼ cup extra-virgin olive oil
- 2 garlic cloves, peeled and minced (see page 16)
- ¼ teaspoon red pepper flakes
- 1 tablespoon minced fresh parsley or basil (optional)

GATHER COOKING EQUIPMENT

- Large bowl
- Wooden spoon
- Colander
- Plastic wrap
- Large saucepan with lid
- Oven mitts
- 12-inch nonstick skillet

START COOKING!

1. DAY 1 Add 4 cups water and 2¼ teaspoons salt to large bowl. Use wooden spoon to stir to dissolve salt.

2. Place colander in sink. Add dried beans to colander. Search through beans and pick out any small stones or broken beans and discard. Rinse beans with cold water.

3. Add drained beans to salt water in bowl. Cover bowl with plastic wrap and let beans soak at room temperature for at least 8 hours or up to 24 hours.

4. DAY 2 Return colander to sink. Pour beans into colander and rinse with cold water.

5. In large saucepan, combine drained beans, remaining 1½ teaspoons salt, and remaining 5 cups water. (Return colander to sink for step 8.) Bring to boil over medium-high heat.

6. Reduce heat to medium-low and cook at gentle simmer (small bubbles should break occasionally across surface of water), stirring occasionally with wooden spoon, until beans are barely al dente (tender but still chewy in the middle), 25 to 30 minutes.

7. Turn off heat and cover saucepan with lid. Let beans steep until tender, 5 to 10 minutes.

8. Use oven mitts to remove lid from saucepan. Ask an adult to drain beans in colander set in sink.

9. In 12-inch nonstick skillet, combine oil and garlic. Cook over medium heat until garlic begins to brown lightly at edges, 3 to 4 minutes.

10. Add red pepper flakes and cook for 30 seconds. Add drained cooked beans and stir gently to coat with oil. Cook, stirring occasionally, until heated through, about 2 minutes. Turn off heat. Sprinkle with parsley (if using) and serve.

Make Time to Brine

Dried beans start out as the seeds of a bean plant that grow inside long pods (see page 147). Those seed pods are dried in the sun until the water inside the beans evaporates, making the beans dry and hard. Drying beans this way allows them to last a long time on your pantry shelf.

To turn them tender again, dried beans need to be cooked in liquid, or rehydrated, which can take hours and hours. One way to speed things up? Brine the beans. Soaking dried beans in a saltwater solution—just like we did with chicken (see page 105)—does two things: It softens the beans' skins (the seed coats) and it shortens the time it takes to cook them. The skins of beans contain pectin, a molecule that "glues" plant cells together. As the beans soak in the brine, sodium ions in the dissolved salt weaken the pectin in the beans' skins, making them softer and able to expand (instead of explode) as the beans absorb water. During their time in the brine, the beans start to absorb water, first through their hilia (the little holes on the curved parts of the beans) and eventually through their entire seed coats. This gives the beans a hydrating "jump start" and means you won't have to cook them for quite as long.

BLACK BEAN BURGERS

This flavorful twist on a classic veggie burger has the added "bean"-efit of black beans and Southwestern-inspired seasoning. You will need two 15-ounce cans of black beans to yield 2 cups. Save leftover black beans for another use.

SERVES: 4

TOTAL TIME: 45 minutes

LEVEL:

PREPARE INGREDIENTS

- 1 large egg
- 1 tablespoon chili powder
- ¼ teaspoon salt
- ¼ teaspoon pepper
- 2 ounces tortilla chips, crushed (1 cup)
- 2 cups drained black beans
- 4 scallions, ends trimmed and chopped coarse
- ¼ cup mayonnaise
- ½–1 teaspoon sriracha
- 2 tablespoons vegetable oil
- 1 small head Bibb lettuce (6 ounces), leaves separated
- 4 hamburger buns, toasted

GATHER COOKING EQUIPMENT

- 2 bowls (1 large, 1 small)
- Whisk
- Food processor
- Rubber spatula
- Ruler
- Large plate
- Spoon
- 12-inch nonstick skillet
- Spatula

START COOKING!

1. In large bowl, whisk egg, chili powder, salt, and pepper until well combined.

2. Add tortilla chips to food processor. Lock lid into place. Turn on food processor and process until tortilla chips are very finely ground, about 1 minute. Stop processor.

3. Remove lid and add beans and scallions to processor. Lock lid back into place. Hold down pulse button for 1 second, then release. Repeat until ingredients are finely chopped, 10 to 15 one-second pulses.

4. Remove lid and carefully remove processor blade (ask an adult for help). Transfer black bean mixture to bowl with egg mixture. Use rubber spatula to gently stir ingredients until just combined.

5. Use your wet hands to divide black bean mixture into 4 portions and form 4 lightly packed balls. Gently flatten each ball into circle that measures 3½ inches across (see photo, right). Transfer patties to plate and refrigerate for 10 minutes.

6. Meanwhile, in small bowl, stir mayonnaise and sriracha with spoon until well combined. Set aside.

7. When patties are ready, heat oil in 12-inch nonstick skillet for 1 minute (oil should be hot but not smoking). Carefully place patties in skillet and cook over medium heat until well browned on first side, 4 to 6 minutes.

8. Use spatula to gently flip patties (ask an adult for help). Cook until well browned on second side, 4 to 5 minutes. Turn off heat.

9. Place 1 lettuce leaf onto each bun bottom. Use spatula to slide burgers on top of lettuce leaves. Top with sriracha mayonnaise and bun tops. Serve.

A Can-Do Attitude

The process of getting beans from the plant to the can is a marvel of culinary engineering. First, bean plants are cut down and left to dry out. Then, machines separate the dried beans from their pods. While the exact canning process varies from brand to brand, it usually starts with cleaning the beans, sorting them by size, and removing any beans that are damaged. Then, the dried beans are quickly cooked in hot water before they're sealed in their cans along with water and salt. The salt not only seasons the beans but also makes their skins more tender. Finally, the beans are pressure cooked, right in their cans—no pot required. The result? Perfectly cooked, flavorful beans, ready to use at a moment's notice!

SHAPING BLACK BEAN BURGERS

Use your wet hands to divide black bean mixture into 4 portions and form 4 lightly packed balls. Gently flatten each ball into circle that measures 3½ inches across.

SNACKS & DRINKS

WHY DOES CORN "POP"?

Popcorn: a fluffy, crunchy snack that POPS while it cooks. And that pop has everything to do with popcorn's structure. Every popcorn kernel is surrounded by a hard outer layer called the hull. Inside the kernel you'll find the germ and the endosperm. The endosperm is made of starch, tiny droplets of water, and a bit of protein. As kernels heat up, those tiny droplets of water expand and turn into steam, pushing against the tough hull. When enough pressure builds up inside the kernel the starch BURSTS through the hull and quickly solidifies in the cooler air—kind of like a small, corny balloon. The white-yellow, billowy part of popcorn? That's solidified starch. Learn more about how water can change that pop in our science experiment (page 155), listen to the pop of a batch of Stovetop Popcorn (page 158), and transform the results of all that popping into sweet and crunchy Chocolate-Covered Popcorn (page 160).

A KERNEL OF TRUTH

TOTAL TIME: 45 minutes, plus 8 hours soaking and drying time

LEVEL:

MATERIALS

Masking tape

Marker

2 airtight containers with lids, approximately 16 ounces each

¼-cup dry measuring cup

¾ cup popcorn kernels

¼ cup water

Rimmed baking sheet

Oven mitts

Cooling rack

3 large microwave-safe plates

Paper towels

Colander

3 medium bowls

3 clean paper lunch bags

Measuring spoons

1½ teaspoons vegetable oil

What makes popcorn pop? Does a popcorn kernel with more water pop more . . . or less? Learn why in this corny experiment! Make sure to use plain paper lunch bags without any writing on them (colored inks are often not microwave-safe).

LET'S GO!

1 Use masking tape and marker to label 1 airtight container "Hydrated" and second airtight container "Dehydrated." ("Hydrate" means "to add water" and "dehydrate" means "to take away water.")

2 Add ¼ cup popcorn kernels and water to container labeled "Hydrated." Place lid on container and set aside for at least 8 hours and up to 24 hours.

3 Meanwhile, heat oven to 200 degrees. Add ¼ cup popcorn kernels to rimmed baking sheet and spread into even layer. Place baking sheet in oven. Bake kernels for 2 hours.

4 Use oven mitts to remove baking sheet from oven and place on cooling rack (ask an adult for help). Let popcorn kernels cool completely, about 15 minutes.

5 Transfer popcorn kernels from rimmed baking sheet to airtight container labeled "Dehydrated." Store at room temperature until hydrated popcorn kernels are ready.

KEEP GOING! ↰

DIY MICROWAVE POPCORN

Place plate in microwave and cook until popping slows down to 1 or 2 pops at a time, 3 to 5 minutes. Use oven mitts to remove plate from microwave (ask an adult for help—plate will be very hot).

Eat Your Experiment!

Add 1 tablespoon melted **unsalted butter** to bowl of control popcorn. Use rubber spatula to toss popcorn with butter. Sprinkle with ¼ teaspoon **salt**. Serve.

6 When hydrated popcorn kernels are ready, line 1 large microwave-safe plate with 2 paper towels. Set colander in sink. Pour hydrated kernels into colander. Shake colander to drain well. Transfer drained kernels to paper towel–lined plate. Use another paper towel to blot kernels until dry.

7 Use masking tape and marker to label 1 bowl "Hydrated," second bowl "Dehydrated," and remaining bowl "Control." (Learn more about control samples on page 11.)

8 **MAKE A PREDICTION** What do you think will happen when you pop the hydrated kernels, the dehydrated kernels, and the control kernels? Will the popped popcorn look the same or different? Why?

9 Add remaining ¼ cup popcorn kernels to 1 paper lunch bag. Drizzle kernels with ½ teaspoon oil. Fold over top of bag 3 times to seal (do not tape or staple it). Shake bag to coat kernels evenly with oil, place bag on its side on large microwave-safe plate, and shake kernels into even layer in bag.

10 Place plate in microwave and cook until popping slows down to 1 or 2 pops at a time, 3 to 5 minutes. Use oven mitts to remove plate from microwave (ask an adult for help; see photo, above). Carefully open paper bag (be careful of hot steam) and pour popcorn into bowl labeled "Control."

11 Repeat steps 9 and 10 with hydrated and dehydrated popcorn kernels, using different microwave-safe plate each time.

12 **OBSERVE YOUR RESULTS** Compare your 3 samples. Do they look similar or different? Which bowl is filled up the most? That's the fluffiest popcorn! Taste each sample. Which is your favorite?

STOP UNDERSTANDING YOUR RESULTS
(Don't read until you've completed the experiment!)

Control   Dehydrated   Hydrated

THE BIG IDEAS

- Popcorn kernels contain water. When that water turns into hot steam, it creates pressure inside the kernel and, eventually, causes it to explode into fluffy popcorn.
- The dehydrated kernels contained less water, so there was less steam created during popping, which translated into less fluffy popcorn.
- The hydrated kernels contained too much water, which made the outside of the kernels weak. The kernels popped before much pressure built up, creating flat—not fluffy—popcorn.

In the Recipe Lab, we found that the control popcorn kernels produced the fluffiest popcorn, the dried kernels produced less fluffy popcorn, and the soaked kernels produced hard popcorn that was the opposite of fluffy. All popcorn kernels contain water plus starch and protein (see page 154). When popcorn is cooking, that water turns into hot steam. This creates pressure inside the popcorn kernel, which builds and builds and, eventually, causes the kernel to burst into fluffy popcorn. Changing the amount of water inside the kernel by either soaking or drying it out definitely changed how it popped!

Drying the kernels in the oven caused some of the water inside to evaporate, so less steam built up inside the kernels as they cooked. When a dehydrated kernel finally did pop, there wasn't as much force to make it fluffy. Think about popping a half-blown-up balloon (your dehydrated popcorn) versus popping a fully blown-up balloon (your control popcorn). The fully blown-up balloon would pop with more force, since there's more gas and pressure in the balloon. Same with popcorn.

As the hydrated kernels soaked, water traveled through their hulls into their starchy interiors, making them expand and making the hull weaker. This caused the kernels to pop before much pressure had built up inside the kernel. They made some loud popping sounds in the microwave, but the results were pretty flat—literally!

recipe

STOVETOP POPCORN

To make a big batch of fluffy popcorn, look no further than your saucepan. Heat from the stove at the bottom of the pot causes the popcorn to pop, and a not-quite-closed lid keeps the popcorn inside the pot while allowing steam to escape.

SERVES: 4 to 6
(Makes 10 cups)

TOTAL TIME: 15 minutes

LEVEL: ▲

PREPARE INGREDIENTS

- 1 tablespoon vegetable oil
- ½ cup popcorn kernels

GATHER COOKING EQUIPMENT

- Large saucepan with lid
- Oven mitts
- Large bowl

START COOKING!

1. In large saucepan, combine oil and 3 individual popcorn kernels. Place lid on saucepan slightly to one side, leaving small gap but keeping pot mostly covered (see photo, right).

2. Heat over medium-high heat until kernels pop, 1 to 3 minutes (stand back from pot, oil may splash as kernels pop). Turn off heat and slide saucepan to cool burner.

3. Use oven mitts to remove lid. Add remaining popcorn kernels. Cover pot with lid and let sit for 30 seconds.

4. Place pot over medium heat. Use oven mitts to slide lid slightly to one side, leaving small gap but keeping pot mostly covered. Continue to cook, with lid slightly ajar, until popping slows to about 2 seconds between pops, 1 to 3 minutes. Turn off heat and slide saucepan to cool burner.

5. Use oven mitts to carefully remove lid (steam will be HOT). Transfer popcorn to large bowl. You can flavor your popcorn as desired (see Make It Your Way, below). Serve. (Popcorn can be stored at room temperature in airtight container for up to 1 day.)

Make It Your Way

You can dress up this popcorn lots of different ways to make it just the way you like it. You can keep it simple by drizzling it with 2 tablespoons of **melted butter** and sprinkling it with ¼ teaspoon **salt**, or add ½ cup **grated Parmesan cheese** for a cheesy snack. You can even raid the spice cabinet and add some **spices** or **dried herbs** to your melted butter to flavor it. Start with ¼ to ½ teaspoon of spices or dried herbs and go up from there.

PUT A LID ON IT (MOSTLY)

When making popcorn, keep the saucepan almost (but not all the way!) covered with the lid. This keeps the popcorn inside the pan, but still allows some steam to escape as the popcorn pops.

"Pop" Goes the Popcorn

You know that popcorn explodes thanks to steam (see page 157), but what causes popcorn to make that iconic "pop" sound? Scientists pondered this question for a long time. Was it the sound of the hull (the outside of the kernel) breaking apart? The kernel bursting into the air as it pushed against the pan? A few years ago, a team of scientists in France watched (and listened!) to popcorn pop in superslow motion—and discovered that it was neither of those things. Instead, they discovered that the "pop" is actually the sound of the water vapor—or steam—escaping as the kernel bursts open. The change in pressure inside the kernel right before it bursts causes the teeny-tiny spaces inside the popcorn to vibrate and produce a noise. Talk about good vibrations.

SERVES: 6 to 8 (Makes 7 cups)

TOTAL TIME: 1½ hours, plus cooling time

LEVEL:

recipe

CHOCOLATE-COVERED POPCORN

Take your popped kernels to the next level by coating them with a chocolaty sauce for a sweet-and-salty treat. Only use plain popcorn in this recipe, not popcorn with butter flavoring. Natural unsweetened cocoa powder works best; Dutch-processed cocoa powder makes the sauce too grainy.

PREPARE INGREDIENTS

   Vegetable oil spray

 7 cups popped plain popcorn (see page 158 or use store-bought)

 5 tablespoons unsalted butter

 ¾ cup (5¼ ounces) sugar

 ¼ cup light corn syrup

 3 tablespoons unsweetened cocoa powder

 ¼ teaspoon salt

 ¼ teaspoon baking soda

 1 teaspoon flake sea salt (optional)

GATHER COOKING EQUIPMENT

 13-by-9-inch metal baking pan

 Aluminum foil

 Large saucepan

 Rubber spatula

 Oven mitts

 Cooling rack

START COOKING!

1. Adjust oven rack to middle position and heat oven to 250 degrees. Line 13-by-9-inch metal baking pan with aluminum foil. Spray inside bottom and sides of pan with vegetable oil spray. Place popcorn in baking pan.

2. In large saucepan, melt butter over medium-high heat. Add sugar, corn syrup, cocoa powder, and ¼ teaspoon salt and bring mixture to boil.

3. Reduce heat to medium-low and cook, stirring constantly with rubber spatula, until sugar dissolves and mixture is smooth, about 1 minute.

4. Turn off heat and slide saucepan to cool burner. Carefully add baking soda and stir until well combined, about 30 seconds.

5. Working quickly, while mixture is still hot, ask an adult to use rubber spatula to carefully scrape sauce mixture onto popcorn in baking pan (saucepan will be heavy and sauce will be hot). Use rubber spatula to gently stir until popcorn is evenly coated. Spread popcorn into even layer. Sprinkle with flake sea salt (if using).

6. Place baking pan in oven and bake for 20 minutes.

7. Use oven mitts to remove baking pan from oven and place on cooling rack (ask an adult for help). Use rubber spatula to carefully stir popcorn, scraping up sauce from bottom of pan (pan will be hot). Spread popcorn back into even layer.

8. Use oven mitts to return baking pan to oven. Bake until chocolate coating has hardened, about 40 minutes, repeating stirring halfway through baking.

9. Use oven mitts to remove baking pan from oven and place on cooling rack (ask an adult for help). Carefully stir popcorn one last time. Let popcorn cool completely in pan, about 30 minutes. Break popcorn apart with your hands and serve.

"Pop" Quiz: Popcorn Shapes

There are two basic popcorn shapes: butterfly (also called snowflake) and mushroom. Most of the popcorn you get at the grocery store or movie theater is butterfly popcorn. Butterfly popcorn is light and fluffy and looks like it has little "wings" popping out of it. In fact, the popcorn industry sorts those popped kernels into three categories based on which way the wings pop. Unilateral pieces of popcorn have wings in only one direction, bilateral pieces of popcorn expand in two directions, and multilateral pieces of popcorn expand in three or more directions. Mushroom popcorn has a rounder shape without wings and a thicker, chewier texture. You can use either in this recipe, but butterfly popcorn will be easier to find.

Butterfly

Mushroom

CAN YOU TELL THE DIFFERENCE BETWEEN CRISPY AND CRUNCHY?

When you eat, the texture of food can play a big role in what you think of its flavor. Mushy pasta? No thanks. Lumpy pudding? No way! But tender pasta and smooth pudding? More, please.

In this chapter, we're going to dive into two very specific textures: crispy and crunchy. Are they the same? If not, how can you tell the difference? In this case, the texture has to do with both how it feels in your mouth and how it sounds when you eat.

Dive into the different textures and sounds in our science experiment (page 163), and then make CRUNCHY tortilla chips (page 168) and CRISPY frico chips (page 170).

THE BATTLE OF
CRISPY VERSUS CRUNCHY

Scientists have been exploring what makes foods crispy or crunchy for decades—now it's your turn! In this experiment, you'll determine whether chips and crackers are crispy or crunchy. In part 1 you'll gather data using your senses. In part 2 you'll measure how much force it takes to break each chip or cracker. You can use some of your homemade Corn Tortilla Chips (page 168) in this experiment, if desired.

TOTAL TIME: 20 minutes

LEVEL:

MATERIALS

Sheet of paper

Pencil

3 wide, thin, and crispy or crunchy snack foods, such as:

> Potato chips
>
> Kettle chips
>
> Pringles potato crisps
>
> Tortilla chips
>
> Doritos chips
>
> Saltines
>
> Water crackers

Digital kitchen scale

2 small paper or plastic cups, about 3 ounces each, both the same size

Pen with rounded cap or pencil with rounded eraser

LET'S GO!

Part 1: Listen

Scientists agree that crispy foods and crunchy foods sound different when we eat them. In the 1970s and 1980s, researchers at the University of Minnesota discovered that people describe foods that make higher-pitched sounds when they chew them as crispy and foods that make lower-pitched sounds when they chew them as crunchy. Examples of high-pitched sounds are squeaky sneakers on a basketball court, a kitten's meow, and a mosquito's buzz. Some low-pitched sounds are a lion's roar, a car's engine, and tuba music.

1 **MAKE A PREDICTION** Crispy and crunchy are two words that are often used interchangeably to describe food texture, but they actually mean different things. Which of your snack foods do you think are crispy? Which do you think are crunchy? Why do you think so?

KEEP GOING! ↷

Use pen cap or pencil eraser to gently press on the center of chip or cracker. As slowly as you can, press down harder and harder until chip or cracker breaks.

2 Use sheet of paper and pencil to create a recording sheet for your results. Draw line down center of paper to create 2 columns. Label 1 column "Crispy" and second column "Crunchy."

3 **OBSERVE YOUR RESULTS** Find a quiet space. Eat 1 or 2 of each chip or cracker. As you chew, pay attention to what it sounds like: Does it sound crispy (higher pitched) or crunchy (lower pitched)? Based on your observations, write the name of each chip or cracker in the "Crispy" or "Crunchy" column on your sheet of paper.

Part 2: Measure

Use a scale to measure how much force it takes to break each chip or cracker. The amount of force tells you how hard you would have to push down with your teeth to bite through the food. We highly recommend having an adult or friend help you with this experiment. One person can push down on the chip or cracker until it breaks. The other person can observe the reading on the scale.

1 Before you begin, use a pencil to write the name of each chip or cracker on the back of your sheet of paper.

2 Set digital kitchen scale to measure ounces. Place 2 small paper or plastic cups upside down on scale. Lay single chip or cracker across cups (like a bridge). Press "tare" or "zero" button on scale. It should now show zero weight.

3 While an adult or friend watches scale to record reading, use pen cap or pencil eraser to gently press on center of chip or cracker (see photo, page 164). As slowly as you can, press down harder and harder until chip or cracker breaks. Record reading on scale when chip or cracker breaks next to its name on your paper. (If it takes A LOT of force to break a chip or cracker, you might max out how much force your scale can measure—record "max" as your data point for that food.)

---

4 **OBSERVE YOUR RESULTS** Repeat test 3 times with each type of chip or cracker, recording readings on scale next to each chip or cracker's name.

---

5 Look at the data you recorded on your sheet of paper: Which chips or crackers took the most force to break? Which chips or crackers took the least force to break? Did the foods that took the most force to break sound high pitched or low pitched? What other patterns did you notice?

KEEP GOING! ⤵

> "My favorite test was the 2nd test, the one with the force. I learned that Lays chips are crispy, I didn't know that until I did the tests."
> —WILL, AGE 9

UNDERSTANDING YOUR RESULTS
(Don't read until you've completed the experiment!)

THE BIG IDEAS

- Crispy foods sound higher pitched as we chew them while crunchy foods sound lower pitched.
- Crispy foods tend to be thinner and more delicate. Crunchy foods are thicker and sturdier.
- In general, it takes less force to bite through a crispy food than a crunchy food.

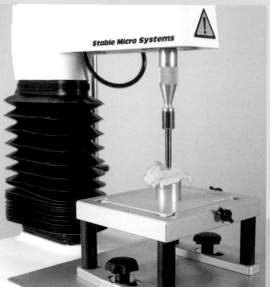

TEXTURE TECHNOLOGIES CORP., HAMILTON, MA

In the Recipe Lab, we noticed that crispy foods took less force to break and tended to be thinner and lighter. Crunchy foods took more force to break and were thicker and sturdier. Crispy foods sounded higher pitched when we ate them while crunchy foods sounded lower pitched. How about you?

According to scientists, crispy foods tend to be hard but delicate—they shatter easily, like a potato chip. Crunchy foods tend to be thicker and make a crushing noise when you chew them, like a tortilla chip or cracker. Whether we think a food is crispy or crunchy involves two of our senses: touch and hearing. The sound a food makes when we eat it has a big impact on what we think of its texture. When scientists are studying the texture of different foods—like you just did!—they use two different kinds of tests.

First is sensory analysis: A group of people use their senses (touch, sight, smell, taste, hearing) to rate different properties of food. You did some sensory analysis when you compared the sounds of eating different foods. This kind of testing is subjective: Each person gives their own opinion, so everyone's answers might be slightly different.

Second is texture analysis: Special machines measure different properties of foods, such as the crispiness of a potato chip or the softness of a muffin. You did a kind of texture analysis when you measured how much force it took to break each food. This kind of testing is objective: No opinions are involved, just measurements and numbers.

Scientists use a combination of sensory analysis AND texture analysis to help them understand what people like and don't like about different foods. Sensory analysis tells us what people experience when they're eating. Texture analysis gives us details on the exact properties of different foods, such as crunchiness and chewiness. Machines can measure these properties much better than people—and since they don't eat, there aren't any foods they don't like!

CORN TORTILLA CHIPS

Chunky or smooth salsas and dips taste great when scooped up with these CRUNCHY tortilla chips. You can use these tortilla chips in The Battle of Crispy versus Crunchy (page 163), if desired.

SERVES: 4 (Makes 36 chips)

TOTAL TIME: 40 minutes

LEVEL:

PREPARE INGREDIENTS

Vegetable oil spray

6 (6-inch) corn tortillas

¼ teaspoon salt

GATHER COOKING EQUIPMENT

Rimmed baking sheet

Cutting board

Chef's knife

Oven mitts

Cooling rack

> **"It tasted even better than the store-bought chips! I loved that I could eat them warm."**
> —SHEVY, 13

Munchable, Crunchable Corn Tortilla Chips

Corn tortillas start out as a moist dough—called masa—that's flattened and cooked on a hot griddle. To turn soft, flexible tortillas into hard, crunchy tortilla chips, we first need to get rid of as much water as possible. As the tortilla wedges bake, the heat in the oven turns much of their water into steam, which evaporates into the surrounding air. The other secret to these crunchy chips? Vegetable oil. The layer of oil on the surface of the tortilla wedges doesn't evaporate in the hot oven. Instead, the oil absorbs the oven's heat and helps the chips' surface get even hotter. This encourages even more water evaporation and helps the chips' surface turn golden brown. Enter your finished tortilla chips in The Battle of Crispy versus Crunchy (page 163) to see whether they live up to their crunchy expectation.

START COOKING!

1. Adjust oven rack to lower-middle position and heat oven to 350 degrees. Spray rimmed baking sheet with vegetable oil spray.

2. Place tortillas on cutting board. Cut each tortilla in half. Cut each tortilla half into 3 equal wedges. Place tortilla wedges on greased baking sheet, in a single layer, alternating point up and point down, so they fit on baking sheet (see photo, right).

3. Spray tortilla wedges generously with vegetable oil spray. Make sure wedges are evenly coated and shiny. Sprinkle salt evenly over tortilla wedges.

4. Place baking sheet in oven. Bake until chips are golden on edges, 12 to 15 minutes.

5. Use oven mitts to remove baking sheet from oven and place on cooling rack (ask an adult for help). Let chips cool on baking sheet for 10 minutes. Serve. (Chips can be stored at room temperature in airtight container for up to 4 days.)

ARRANGING CHIPS TO FIT

Place tortilla wedges on greased baking sheet, in a single layer, alternating point up and point down so that they fit on baking sheet.

recipe

FRICO CHIPS

Move over melty and gooey cheese! These cheesy chips are a CRISPY, savory snack. Be sure to shred the Asiago cheese on the large holes of a box grater.

SERVES: 4 (Makes 20 chips)

TOTAL TIME: 35 minutes

LEVEL:

PREPARE INGREDIENTS

Vegetable oil spray

¾ cup shredded Asiago cheese (1½ ounces)

GATHER COOKING EQUIPMENT

Rimmed baking sheet

Parchment paper

1-teaspoon measuring spoon

Ruler

Oven mitts

Cooling rack

Thin metal spatula

Serving plate

START COOKING!

1. Adjust oven rack to middle position and heat oven to 350 degrees. Line rimmed baking sheet with parchment paper. Spray parchment paper with vegetable oil spray.

2. Use 1-teaspoon measuring spoon to shape and press cheese into twenty 2-inch circles following photo, right.

3. Place baking sheet in oven. Bake until cheese turns light golden brown, 9 to 11 minutes.

4. Use oven mitts to remove baking sheet from oven and place on cooling rack (ask an adult for help). Let chips cool for 10 minutes.

5. Use thin metal spatula to carefully lift frico off parchment paper and transfer to serving plate. Serve. (Frico can be stored at room temperature in airtight container for up to 3 days.)

SHAPING FRICO CHIPS

Use 1-teaspoon measuring spoon to scoop and drop shredded cheese onto parchment paper–lined baking sheet in 20 mounds (about 1 heaping teaspoon each). Use your fingers to gently press each mound into 2-inch-wide circle.

Crispy Cheese?

It takes just one ingredient to create crispy, golden frico ("FREE-koh"): cheese. But you can't use just any cheese to make frico. It has to be a hard, aged cheese, such as Asiago. Don't worry, we don't mean "aged" like your grandparents, or like cheese that's been sitting in your refrigerator for months. In the cheese world, "aged" means that the cheese has spent time—from a few months to more than a year—sitting in a climate-controlled room before it's packaged to sell. As a cheese ages, it loses water through evaporation and becomes harder. Aged cheeses are also more flavorful—bonus!

When you melt an aged cheese such as Asiago, it dries out quickly (because it has less water to start with) and then becomes crispy and golden brown. If you tried to make frico with a young cheese, such as Monterey Jack, which contains more water, it wouldn't work. Monterey Jack gets soft and gooey when you heat it, rather than brown and crispy.

WHY DO SOME FRUITS *turn* BROWN

WHEN YOU LEAVE THEM OUT?

When you slice an apple or peach, peel a banana, or cut open an avocado and then leave the fruit out, air touches the flesh inside. After a few minutes or hours, it will start to turn brown—yuck!

Many fruits and vegetables, such as apples, pears, bananas, potatoes, and avocados start to turn brown once they're cut or bruised and their flesh is exposed to oxygen in the air. This is known as enzymatic ("en-zih-MAT-tic") browning.

But worry not, there are ways to prevent that brown color. You can test them yourselves in our science experiment (page 173), Chunky Guacamole (page 176), and Fruit Salad with Vanilla and Mint (page 178). What's your favorite way to keep your fruit fresh and bright?

APPLE-Y EVER AFTER

TOTAL TIME: 1¾ hours

LEVEL:

MATERIALS

- Masking tape
- Marker
- 5 small bowls
- Liquid measuring cup
- Water
- 2 tablespoons honey
- 2 tablespoons lemon juice, squeezed from 1 lemon
- ¾ teaspoon salt
- Spoon
- Cutting board
- Chef's knife
- 1 Granny Smith or Red Delicious apple
- Paper towels
- Dish towel

Like lots of pesky fruits, apples start to turn brown once you cut them. Is there a way to keep their color if you want to take your apple slices on the go? In this experiment you'll test a few antibrowning remedies and find out which works best. This experiment works best with a Red Delicious or Granny Smith apple—they both brown easily.

LET'S GO!

1 Use masking tape and marker to label 5 small bowls "Water," "Honey," "Lemon," "Salt," and "Control." (See page 11 to learn more about control samples in experiments.)

2 Add 1 cup water each to "Water," "Honey," "Lemon," and "Salt" bowls. Add honey to "Honey" bowl, lemon juice to "Lemon" bowl, and salt to "Salt" bowl. Use spoon to stir each bowl until well combined, rinsing spoon between bowls.

3 Slice apple following photo, page 174.

4 Add 3 apple slices to each bowl. Cover each bowl of apples, including "Control" bowl, with folded paper towel. Gently press paper towel into apples in each bowl to submerge them in water. Leave paper towel in place. Let apple slices soak for 5 minutes.

KEEP GOING! ↷

QUESTION 18
FRUIT

HOW TO SLICE AN APPLE

Use chef's knife to slice around apple core to remove 4 large pieces. Place 1 piece flat side down on cutting board. Cut into ½-inch-thick slices. Repeat with remaining apple pieces.

5 **MAKE A PREDICTION** Which do you think will work the best for preventing the apple slices from turning brown: water, honey, lemon juice, or salt? Why do you think so?

6 When apple slices are ready, remove and discard paper towels. Working with 1 bowl at a time, remove apple slices and set aside. Discard any liquid in bowl and dry bowl with dish towel. Return apple slices to bowl. Repeat with remaining bowls.

7 **OBSERVE YOUR RESULTS** Observe your apple slices every 15 minutes for 1 hour. Are any of the apples turning brown? Which ones?

8 Taste 1 apple slice from each bowl. What do you notice about each apple's flavor? Its texture? Which is your favorite?

STOP UNDERSTANDING YOUR RESULTS
(Don't read until you've completed the experiment!)

THE BIG IDEAS

- Many vegetables and fruits turn brown when they are cut or bruised and their flesh is exposed to air. This is caused by a chemical reaction known as enzymatic browning.
- Enzymes in the apple speed up a reaction between oxygen in the air and compounds in the fruit. That reaction produces new, brown-colored compounds.
- Soaking sliced apples in a mixture of honey and water or salt and water works best to prevent browning.

In the Recipe Lab, we discovered that the apples soaked in the saltwater and the honey-water mixture were barely browned at all, even after an hour had passed. The apple slices soaked in the lemon juice–water mixture did turn brown after 60 minutes—but not as brown as the apple slices soaked in plain water and the control apple slices, which started to brown very quickly.

Many fruits and vegetables start to turn brown once their flesh is exposed to oxygen in the air. This is known as enzymatic ("en-zih-MAT-tic") browning. Enzymes are proteins that help other molecules undergo chemical reactions. In the case of our apple slices, enzymes speed up a reaction between oxygen in the air and molecules in the fruit. That reaction produces new, brown-colored compounds. While it's difficult to stop enzymatic browning from happening altogether, there are techniques that can slow it down.

Using a mixture of honey or salt and water helps keep browning at bay. Both honey and salt get in the way of the enzymes involved in the browning reactions. Mixing the salt and honey with water mellows out their flavor and texture (you won't end up with supersticky or salty apples). Plus, submerging the slices in water slows down browning because not as much oxygen can reach the apple's flesh (but don't leave them in water for too long; they'll get mushy). Certain acids, such as the ones in lemon juice, also get in the way of those enzymes and slow down the browning reaction, but you need a lot of acid to prevent browning—and that would make your apple slices taste really, really sour.

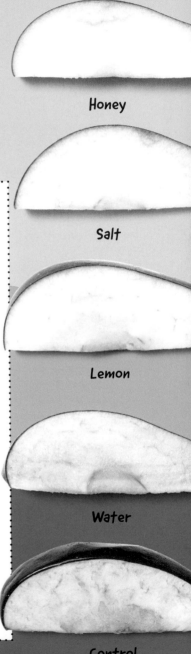

Honey

Salt

Lemon

Water

Control

CHUNKY GUACAMOLE

It's important to use Hass avocados for this recipe. Florida, or "skinny," avocados are too watery for dips. Chiles contain a compound called capsaicin that makes them spicy. To make sure you do not get capsaicin on your skin or in your eyes, make sure to wear disposable gloves when touching chiles like jalapeños.

MAKES about 2 cups
(Serves 8)

TOTAL TIME 25 minutes

LEVEL:

PREPARE INGREDIENTS

- 2 tablespoons onion, finely chopped (see page 16)

- ½ jalapeño, stemmed, halved, seeded, and minced (see page 17)

- 1 garlic clove, peeled and minced (see page 16)

- 1 teaspoon kosher salt

- ¼ teaspoon grated lime zest plus 2 tablespoons juice, zested and squeezed from 1 lime (see page 15)

- 3 ripe Hass avocados

- 1 plum tomato, cored and chopped

- 2 tablespoons chopped fresh cilantro (see page 15)

GATHER COOKING EQUIPMENT

Cutting board

Chef's knife

Spoon

Medium bowl

Butter knife

Whisk

Rubber spatula

START COOKING!

1. Place onion, jalapeño, garlic, salt, and lime zest on cutting board in a small pile. Place one hand on handle of chef's knife and rest fingers of your other hand on top of blade. Chop vegetables, using rocking motion and pivoting knife as you chop, until vegetables are very finely minced (mixture will look like a paste; see photo, right).

2. Use spoon to transfer onion mixture to medium bowl. Add lime juice and stir to combine.

3. Cut avocados in half around pit, remove pit, and scoop avocado from skins on to cutting board following photo, below. Cut avocados into ½-inch pieces.

4. Add avocado chunks to bowl with onion mixture. Use whisk to mash and stir until well combined with some ¼-inch to ½-inch chunks of avocado remaining.

5. Add tomato and cilantro to bowl and use rubber spatula to stir until well combined. Serve.

Amazing Acid

The lime juice in this recipe has two very important jobs: First, it adds a bright, tangy flavor and, second, it keeps our guacamole bright green. Avocados are one of those fruits with flesh that turns brown when it's exposed to oxygen, in a process called oxidation (see page 175). So, they need a little help to stay green. Acid to the rescue! One of the acids in lime juice—as well as other citrus juices, such as lemon and orange juice—is a kind of molecule called an antioxidant. "Anti" means "against" and "oxi" means "oxygen," so antioxidants are molecules that help to prevent the oxidation reaction that turns avocados brown.

A PASTE YOU CAN EAT!

We chop the already-minced onion, jalapeño, lime zest, and garlic with a sprinkle of coarse kosher salt to release their flavors and help them mix evenly in the guacamole. Place one hand on handle of chef's knife and rest fingers of your other hand on top of blade. Chop vegetables, using rocking motion and pivoting knife as you chop, until vegetables are very finely minced to a paste.

CUTTING AVOCADOS

Use butter knife to cut avocado in half lengthwise around pit. With your hands, twist both halves in opposite directions to separate. Use spoon to remove pit. Scoop avocado from skins onto cutting board; discard pits and skins. Repeat with remaining avocados.

recipe

FRUIT SALAD WITH VANILLA AND MINT

SERVES: 4
(Makes about 5 cups)

TOTAL TIME: 35 minutes

LEVEL: ▲

Sugar does double duty in this fancy fruit salad: It adds sweetness and prevents the fruit from turning brown. Bartlett pears can be substituted for peaches. Blueberries or raspberries can be substituted for blackberries.

- 2 tablespoons minced fresh mint (see page 15)
- 4 teaspoons sugar
- ¼ teaspoon vanilla extract
- 2 peaches, pitted and cut into ½-inch chunks (see photos, page 179)
- 2 ripe bananas, peeled and sliced into ¼-inch-thick rounds
- 1 cup (5 ounces) blackberries
- 1 tablespoon lime juice, squeezed from 1 lime (see page 15)

GATHER COOKING EQUIPMENT

- Large bowl
- Rubber spatula

START COOKING!

1. In large bowl, combine mint and sugar. Use rubber spatula to mash and press mixture into side of bowl until sugar is moistened, about 30 seconds. Stir in vanilla.

2. Add peaches, bananas, and blackberries to bowl with sugar mixture. Use rubber spatula to toss fruit gently until coated with sugar mixture. Let stand at room temperature, stirring occasionally, until fruit releases its juices, about 15 minutes.

3. Gently stir in lime juice. Serve.

Sweet Protection

Sugar doesn't just make this fruit salad taste sweet. It also helps to keep the bananas and peaches from turning brown. (Is there anything worse than a mushy brown banana in a fruit salad? Well, yes. But not a whole lot.) When you add sugar to fruit, the sugar pulls water from inside the fruit's cells (where there is more of it) to the outside of the fruit's cells (where there is less of it) through osmosis (see page 11). This water mixes with the fruit juices and sugar to make a tasty sweet syrup that coats the fruit in the salad, forming a barrier between the fruit and the air. Because the oxygen in the air is what helps to create this browning reaction (see page 175), when the oxygen can't reach the fruit as well (such as with the syrup barrier here), there isn't any browning!

PITTING AND CUTTING PEACHES

1 Place peaches on cutting board. Cut small slice off bottom of each peach to create flat surface.

2 Slice around pit of each peach to remove 4 large pieces.

3 Cut large peach pieces into wedges that are roughly ½ inch thick. Cut wedges crosswise into ½-inch chunks.

WHAT MAKES FIZZY THINGS Fizzy?

Fizzy drinks are fun to sip, but how do all of those bubbles get into your beverage? The bubbles in seltzer or soda are made of carbon dioxide gas. When seltzer is in a sealed bottle, the gas is dissolved in the liquid—you can't see it. When you open the bottle, some of the dissolved carbon dioxide turns back into a gas and escapes as bubbles. There are all sorts of things you can do to change the amount and speed of the bubbling—from adding nucleation sites (see page 183) to changing temperatures (see page 185). Explore this in our science experiment (page 181), and in recipes for Sparkling Pink Lemonade (page 184) and Ginger Ale (page 186).

BUBBLE TROUBLE

Have you ever noticed that before you open it, you can't see any bubbles in a bottle of soda or seltzer? They only appear once you open the bottle and take a drink or pour the liquid into a glass. In this experiment, you'll learn where those bubbles come from by dropping two different objects—a smooth marble and a rough raisin—into glasses of seltzer and observing what happens.

LET'S GO!

1 **MAKE A PREDICTION** Which glass of seltzer do you think will have more bubbles, the one with the marble or the one with the raisin? Why do you think so?

2 Fill both drinking glasses with cold seltzer until they are about ¾ full (be sure to fill both glasses to the same level).

3 Place glasses side by side on counter. Hold marble about 1 inch above surface of seltzer in 1 glass. Hold raisin about 1 inch above surface of seltzer in second glass (make sure marble and raisin are at same height, see photo, page 182).

4 **OBSERVE YOUR RESULTS** Let go of marble and raisin at same time, letting them drop into their respective glasses. Observe what happens for 30 seconds.

KEEP GOING! ↷

TOTAL TIME: 10 minutes

LEVEL:

MATERIALS

2 tall, clear drinking glasses, both the same size and shape

3 cups (24 ounces) cold seltzer water

1 clean marble or ball bearing

2 raisins or dried cranberries

Spoon

READY, SET, FIZZ!

Hold the marble about 1 inch above the surface of the seltzer in 1 glass. Hold the raisin about 1 inch above the surface of the seltzer in the other glass. You can also enlist a friend for this experiment—1 person can hold the marble and the other person can hold the raisin.

5 Use spoon to retrieve marble and raisin from glasses. Repeat steps 3 and 4 with marble and second raisin. This time, observe what happens for at least 5 minutes. How do your results compare with your prediction from step 1?

UNDERSTANDING YOUR RESULTS

(Don't read until you've completed the experiment!)

THE BIG IDEAS

- The bubbles in seltzer and soda are made of carbon dioxide gas. In a sealed bottle, the gas is dissolved in the liquid—you can't see it.
- To become a bubble, dissolved carbon dioxide gas needs a nucleation site, which can be anything from a speck of dust in a glass to your marble or raisin.
- The wrinkly raisin has more nucleation sites than the smooth marble, so it creates more bubbles right away. The marble creates fewer bubbles, but it makes the liquid bubbly for a longer time.

Fewer nucleation sites = Fewer bubbles for longer

More nucleation sites = More bubbles right away

When we embarked on this effervescent experiment in the Recipe Lab, we observed lots of bubbles right away in the glass with the raisin. There were fewer bubbles in the glass with the marble, but we observed bubbles for a longer time.

As we've learned (see page 180), the bubbles in seltzer or soda are made of carbon dioxide gas. When seltzer is in a sealed bottle, the gas is dissolved in the liquid—you can't see it. When you open the bottle, some of the dissolved carbon dioxide turns back into a gas and escapes as bubbles. But to get the bubbles really popping, you need some help.

Just like Clark Kent needs a phone booth to change into Superman, dissolved carbon dioxide needs a special place to become a bubble, called a nucleation ("new-clee-AY-shun") site. Bubbles form at nucleation sites and rise through the beverage until they pop at the surface. A nucleation site can be anything from a tiny fiber from a towel to a speck of dust to the surfaces of the marble and raisin.

The wrinkly raisin has more nucleation sites than the smooth marble. And more nucleation sites means more bubbles. But there's only so much carbon dioxide dissolved in the seltzer water. Eventually, the bubbles slow down because there's not much carbon dioxide left. The gas is used up more quickly when there are more nucleation sites, as in the glass with the raisin. In the glass with the smooth marble, there were fewer bubbles at any given moment, but the seltzer stayed bubbly for longer.

recipe

SPARKLING PINK LEMONADE

Berries give this sweet-tart lemonade its pink color and cold seltzer water adds maximum bubbles.

SERVES: 8 (Makes about 1½ cups pink lemonade syrup)

TOTAL TIME: 25 minutes

LEVEL:

PREPARE INGREDIENTS

PINK LEMONADE SYRUP

- 5 lemons
- ¾ cup (3¾ ounces) fresh or frozen-and-thawed raspberries, blackberries, and/or strawberries
- ¾ cup sugar

SPARKLING PINK LEMONADE

- Ice
- ¾ cup cold plain seltzer water

GATHER COOKING EQUIPMENT

Cutting board

Chef's knife

2 medium bowls

Potato masher

Citrus juicer

Liquid measuring cup

Rubber spatula

Fine-mesh strainer

Jar with tight-fitting lid

Glass

1-tablespoon measuring spoon

Spoon

START COOKING!

1. FOR THE PINK LEMONADE SYRUP Cut 1 lemon into thin semicircles following photo, right; discard ends.

2. In medium bowl, combine lemon slices, berries, and sugar. Use potato masher to mash until berries are broken down and sugar is completely wet, about 1 minute; set aside.

3. Cut remaining 4 lemons in half crosswise (the short way). Use citrus juicer to squeeze juice into liquid measuring cup. You should have about ¾ cup juice. (Save any extra juice for another use.)

4. Pour lemon juice into bowl with lemon-berry mixture. Use rubber spatula to stir until sugar is completely dissolved, about 1 minute.

5. Set fine-mesh strainer over second medium bowl. Carefully pour mixture through strainer. Use rubber spatula to press on lemons and berries to get out as much juice as possible. Discard lemon slices and berries in strainer.

6. Pour strained pink lemonade syrup into jar with tight-fitting lid. (Pink lemonade syrup can be refrigerated for up to 1 week.)

7. TO MAKE 1 SPARKLING PINK LEMONADE
Stir or shake pink lemonade syrup to recombine. Place ice in glass. Pour cold seltzer into glass over ice. Add 3 tablespoons pink lemonade syrup to seltzer. Use spoon to stir gently to combine. Serve.

SLICING LEMONS

Cut 1 lemon in half lengthwise through both ends. Lay lemon halves, flat side down, on cutting board, then cut each half crosswise into thin semicircles.

To Keep Your Sparkle, Keep It Cold!

Chilling your seltzer water and serving lemonade over ice doesn't just keep the drink cold, it also keeps bubbles in your glass for longer! Seltzer water is made fizzy by adding carbon dioxide gas to water while it's under pressure. Once a can or bottle of seltzer is opened (and no longer under pressure), that gas will escape into the air. Warmer mixtures let gas escape more quickly, meaning your fizzy drink will soon become flat if it's too warm. Fun fact: Scientists have found that cold carbonated drinks make you feel less thirsty when you drink them!

recipe

GINGER ALE

Fresh ginger brings a new level of flavor to this bubbly soda fountain favorite. Because this recipe skips peeling the ginger, make sure to wash and dry it well before slicing.

SERVES: 6 (Makes about 1½ cups ginger syrup)

TOTAL TIME: 50 minutes

LEVEL: ▲

PREPARE INGREDIENTS

GINGER SYRUP

4 ounces fresh ginger

1½ cups water

½ cup sugar

½ cup honey

Pinch salt

¼ cup lime juice, squeezed from 2 limes (see page 15)

GINGER ALE

Ice

¾ cup cold plain seltzer water

GATHER COOKING EQUIPMENT

Cutting board

Chef's knife

Medium saucepan

Wooden spoon

Fine-mesh strainer

Cheesecloth

Medium bowl

Jar with tight-fitting lid

Glass

Spoon

Before sodas were available in cans or bottles, they were made one at a time by a server at a soda fountain, or a counter in a shop (often a pharmacy) that served carbonated drinks. "Soda jerks," as the servers were called, would mix up flavored syrups and then add water that was carbonated by a machine with a tank of carbon dioxide gas inside. Today, sodas are usually manufactured in bottling plants, but the process remains similar. Manufacturers mix up huge batches of syrup, add water, chill everything down until it's very cold, then inject the mixture with carbon dioxide gas while it's under pressure. That mixture is sealed inside bottles or cans, keeping all of the carbon dioxide gas inside, ensuring that your drink will be bubbly whenever you pop it open.

START COOKING!

1. FOR THE GINGER SYRUP Slice ginger crosswise ¼ inch thick (see photo, below). You should have about 1 cup sliced ginger.

2. In medium saucepan, combine sliced ginger, water, sugar, honey, and salt. Bring to simmer over medium heat (small bubbles should break often across surface of mixture).

3. Reduce heat to medium-low and cook, stirring occasionally with wooden spoon, for 15 minutes. Turn off heat and slide saucepan to cool burner.

4. Stir in lime juice. Let mixture cool completely, about 30 minutes.

5. Line fine-mesh strainer with triple layer of cheesecloth. Place strainer over medium bowl. Pour cooled ginger mixture through strainer into bowl, pressing gently on ginger pieces to extract as much liquid as possible. Discard cheesecloth and ginger pieces. Pour strained ginger syrup into jar with tight-fitting lid. (Ginger syrup can be refrigerated for up to 1 week.)

6. TO MAKE 1 GINGER ALE Stir or shake ginger syrup to recombine. Place ice in glass. Pour cold seltzer into glass over ice. Add ¼ cup ginger syrup to seltzer. Use spoon to stir gently to combine. Serve.

HOW TO SLICE GINGER

Place ginger on cutting board. Use chef's knife to cut ginger crosswise into slices about ¼ inch thick.

SWEETS

WHAT MAKES SOME COOKIES CHEWY AND SOME CRISP?

Cookies come in different shapes, sizes, flavors, colors, and textures. Here, we're going to focus on textures—crispy and chewy, to be exact.

The ingredients you use and how you shape your cookies both play an important role in whether your cookies turn out crispy or chewy. The type of flour and sugar you use, if your cookie dough contains eggs, and whether you use melted or softened butter all factor into the vcrispy-chewy equation, too.

In the science experiment on page 191, explore how brown and white sugar affect the texture and flavor of cookies. And then, of course, make our Crispy Chocolate Chip Cookies on page 194 and our Chewy Chocolate Cookies on page 196 and decide which texture you like better ("both" is an acceptable answer!).

HOW SWEET IT IS

TOTAL TIME: 2 hours, plus cooling time

LEVEL:

MATERIALS

Measure these ingredients TWICE. Put each ingredient in two separate bowls.

1 cup plus 1 tablespoon (5⅓ ounces) all-purpose flour

¼ teaspoon baking soda

¼ teaspoon salt

⅛ teaspoon baking powder

7 tablespoons unsalted butter, melted (see page 13)

1 large egg yolk (see page 14)

1½ teaspoons vanilla extract

Measure these ingredients ONCE.

¾ cup plus 2 tablespoons packed (6⅛ ounces) dark brown sugar

¾ cup plus 2 tablespoons (6⅛ ounces) white granulated sugar

Gather cooking equipment.

2 rimmed baking sheets

Parchment paper

2 bowls (1 large, 1 medium)

Whisk

Rubber spatula

1-tablespoon measuring spoon

Oven mitts

2 cooling racks

Masking tape

Marker

In this experiment, you'll bake two batches of cookies: one made with brown sugar and one made with white sugar. Then, you'll do a taste test to find out whether the kind of sugar you used affects your cookies' flavor and texture.

LET'S GO!

1 **MAKE A PREDICTION** Do you think cookies made with brown sugar will taste the same as or different from cookies made with white sugar? Why do you think so?

---

2 **MAKE COOKIES WITH BROWN SUGAR** Adjust oven rack to middle position and heat oven to 350 degrees. Line rimmed baking sheet with parchment paper.

---

3 In medium bowl, whisk together 1 cup plus 1 tablespoon flour, ¼ teaspoon baking soda, ¼ teaspoon salt, and ⅛ teaspoon baking powder

KEEP GOING! ↷

SHAPING THE COOKIES

Use your slightly wet hands to roll dough into 10 balls (about 2 tablespoons each). Place dough balls on parchment-lined baking sheet, leaving space between balls.

4 In large bowl, whisk brown sugar and 7 tablespoons melted butter until smooth and no lumps remain, about 30 seconds. Add 1 egg yolk and 1½ teaspoons vanilla and whisk until well combined, about 30 seconds.

5 Add flour mixture to sugar mixture and use rubber spatula to stir until just combined and no dry flour is visible, about 1 minute.

6 Use your slightly wet hands to shape 10 cookies, following photo, left.

7 Place baking sheet in oven. Bake cookies until edges are beginning to set but centers are still soft and puffy (cookies will look raw between cracks and seem underdone), 15 to 20 minutes.

8 Use oven mitts to remove baking sheet from oven and place on cooling rack (ask an adult for help). Use masking tape and marker to label cooling rack "Brown Sugar." Let cookies cool completely on baking sheet, about 30 minutes.

9 MAKE COOKIES WITH WHITE SUGAR
While cookies with brown sugar cool, repeat steps 2 through 8 to make cookies with white sugar, using clean bowls, whisk, and rubber spatula. (Don't forget to use white sugar in step 4!) Use masking tape and marker to label second cooling rack "White Sugar." Let cookies cool completely on baking sheet before tasting, about 30 minutes.

10 OBSERVE YOUR RESULTS Do the cookies with brown sugar and cookies with white sugar look the same or different? How so? Taste 1 cookie from each batch. How would you describe the flavor of each cookie? The texture?

STOP UNDERSTANDING YOUR RESULTS
(Don't read until you've completed the experiment!)

THE BIG IDEAS

- Cookies made with brown sugar are moister and chewier, while cookies made with white sugar are drier and crispier.
- Brown sugar contains more water than white sugar, and it's also more flavorful because it contains molasses.

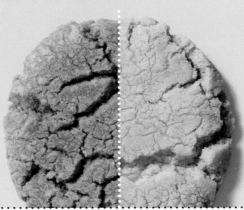

Cookies Made with Brown Sugar

- Darker brown color
- Moister, chewier texture
- Bend easily
- Deep, caramelly flavor
- Thicker and puffier

Cookies Made with White Sugar

- Lighter beige color
- Drier, crispier texture
- Bend a little, then snap
- Mild flavor, taste sweeter
- Thinner and flatter

When we tried this experiment in the Recipe Lab, we observed some big differences between the cookies made with brown sugar and the ones made with white sugar. How about you?

Sugar does more than make cookies sweet—it also affects their texture and their flavor. First things first: Brown sugar is just white sugar with molasses added to it. Molasses gives brown sugar more flavor than white sugar (that's why the two cookies tasted different). It also adds more water to brown sugar. That's one reason the brown sugar cookies had a moister, chewier texture.

Another reason? Sugar is hygroscopic ("hi-grow-SKAH-pick")—it's really good at absorbing and holding on to water from its surroundings. Brown sugar is more hygroscopic than white sugar, which keeps our brown sugar cookies moist and bendable and makes our white sugar cookies crispier.

Finally, thanks to that molasses, brown sugar is a little bit acidic. The acidic molasses reacts with the baking soda in our cookies to produce bubbly carbon dioxide gas, making the brown sugar cookies a bit thicker and puffier than the white sugar cookies.

Lots of cookie recipes call for white and brown sugar. This can give you the best of both worlds in your cookies' texture and flavor. Other recipes use one type of sugar or the other, depending on the flavor and texture they're aiming for. Once you understand this sugary science, the wide world of cookies can be yours!

CRISPY CHOCOLATE CHIP COOKIES

Using just the right ingredients—and a special shaping technique—keeps these cookies crisp. Make sure to use mini chocolate chips in this recipe. We don't recommend substituting regular-size chocolate chips—they'll make the cookies too thick.

MAKES: 12 cookies

TOTAL TIME: 45 minutes, plus cooling time

LEVEL:

PREPARE INGREDIENTS

- ¾ cup (3 ounces) cake flour
- ¼ teaspoon salt
- ⅛ teaspoon baking soda
- 4 tablespoons unsalted butter, melted and cooled (see page 13)
- 3 tablespoons sugar
- 3 tablespoons packed dark brown sugar
- 1 large egg yolk (see page 14)
- 2 teaspoons whole milk
- 1 teaspoon vanilla extract
- ½ cup (3 ounces) mini semisweet chocolate chips
- Vegetable oil spray

GATHER COOKING EQUIPMENT

- Rimmed baking sheet
- Parchment paper
- 2 bowls (1 large, 1 medium)
- Whisk
- Rubber spatula
- 1-tablespoon measuring spoon
- Ruler
- Oven mitts
- Cooling rack

START COOKING!

1. Adjust oven rack to middle position and heat oven to 350 degrees. Line rimmed baking sheet with parchment paper.

2. In medium bowl, whisk together flour, salt, and baking soda.

3. In large bowl, whisk melted butter, sugar, and brown sugar until mixture is very well combined and smooth, about 1 minute. Add egg yolk, milk, and vanilla and whisk until well combined and lightened in color, about 30 seconds.

4. Add flour mixture to melted butter mixture and use rubber spatula to stir until combined and no dry flour is visible. Add chocolate chips and stir until evenly distributed.

5. Spray 1-tablespoon measuring spoon with vegetable oil spray. Use greased measuring spoon to drop dough onto parchment-lined baking sheet in 12 mounds (1 tablespoon each). Respray measuring spoon after every 2 or 3 mounds. Leave space between mounds.

6. Wet your hand lightly and shape cookies following photo, above.

7. Place baking sheet in oven. Bake cookies until golden brown, 12 to 14 minutes.

8. Use oven mitts to remove baking sheet from oven and place on cooling rack (ask an adult for help). Let cookies cool completely on baking sheet, about 30 minutes. Serve.

SHAPING CRISPY COOKIES

Wet your hand lightly. Use your damp hand to gently flatten each mound to 2-inch-wide circle, about ½ inch thick.

Crispy Criteria

To make cookies that are thin and crispy, we picked our ingredients carefully: cake flour, melted butter, egg yolk, and a combination of brown and white sugar. Cake flour contains less protein than all-purpose flour does, so it forms less gluten when it's mixed into a dough (see page 23). Since gluten gives baked goods their structure, a cookie with less gluten will spread out more in the oven. Using melted butter makes for a softer, moister dough that spreads out as it bakes. Like gluten, egg proteins help give baked goods structure. Skipping the protein-packed egg white keeps our cookies thin and crispy. The brown sugar adds molasses-y flavor while the white sugar holds on to less moisture to help with crispness. Last but not least: Pressing these cookies before they go into the oven encourages them to spread out evenly for optimal crispiness!

recipe

CHEWY CHOCOLATE COOKIES

Using the right combination of sugars and shaping techniques guarantees thick and chewy cookies. We prefer Dutch processed cocoa powder in this recipe.

MAKES: 12 cookies

TOTAL TIME: 1½ hours, plus cooling time

LEVEL:

PREPARE INGREDIENTS

- ½ cup (2½ ounces) all-purpose flour

- 2 tablespoons Dutch-processed cocoa powder

- ½ teaspoon baking powder

- ¼ teaspoon salt

- ⅔ cup (4 ounces) semisweet chocolate chips

- 2 tablespoons unsalted butter, softened (see page 13)

- ⅓ cup packed (2⅓ ounces) light brown sugar

- 2 tablespoons sugar

- 1 large egg

- ½ teaspoon vanilla extract

GATHER COOKING EQUIPMENT

- 2 bowls (1 medium, 1 medium microwave-safe)

- Whisk

- Oven mitts

- Rubber spatula

- Electric mixer (stand mixer with paddle attachment or handheld mixer and large bowl)

- Plastic wrap

- Rimmed baking sheet

- Parchment paper

- 1-tablespoon measuring spoon

- Cooling rack

START COOKING!

1. In medium bowl, whisk together flour, cocoa, baking powder, and salt.

2. Place chocolate chips in medium microwave-safe bowl. Heat in microwave at 50 percent power until melted, 2 to 3 minutes. Use oven mitts to remove bowl from microwave. Use rubber spatula to stir chocolate until completely melted and smooth.

3. In bowl of stand mixer (or large bowl if using handheld mixer), combine softened butter, brown sugar, and sugar. If using stand mixer, lock bowl into place and attach paddle to stand mixer. Start mixer on medium speed and beat until well combined, about 1½ minutes. Stop mixer and scrape down bowl.

4. Add egg, vanilla, and melted chocolate. Start mixer on low speed and mix until combined, about 2 minutes. Stop mixer and use rubber spatula to scrape down bowl.

5. Add flour mixture. Start mixer on low speed and mix until combined, about 1 minute. Stop mixer. Remove bowl from stand mixer, if using.

6. Scrape down bowl and stir in any remaining dry flour. Cover bowl with plastic wrap. Let dough sit at room temperature for 30 minutes.

7. Meanwhile, adjust oven rack to middle position and heat oven to 350 degrees. Line rimmed baking sheet with parchment paper.

8. When dough is ready, use your hands to roll dough into 12 balls (about 1 heaping tablespoon each). Place dough balls on parchment-lined baking sheet, leaving space between balls (see photo, below).

9. Place baking sheet in oven. Bake cookies until edges have just begun to set but centers are still very soft, 12 to 14 minutes.

10. Use oven mitts to remove baking sheet from oven and place on cooling rack (ask an adult for help). Let cookies cool completely on baking sheet, about 30 minutes. Serve.

Chewy Choices

Thick cookies are often chewy cookies—and we made recipe choices to create cookies that are nice and thick! First, we use more brown sugar than white sugar: Brown sugar contains more water, so it helps make cookies moister and chewier (see page 193). Next, we let the dough rest for 30 minutes before shaping and baking the cookies. As the dough rests, the flour absorbs some of the water in the dough. The dough's texture thickens up, which means that it won't spread as much in the oven. We don't press these cookies flat before baking, which helps prevent them from spreading and keeps them thicker. Finally, removing the cookies from the oven when they look almost done helps maintain their chewy texture.

STAGGER YOUR COOKIES

Leave 2 inches between balls, arranging them in staggered rows so they don't spread into each other as they bake.

WHAT MAKES WHIPPED CREAM SO FLUFFY?

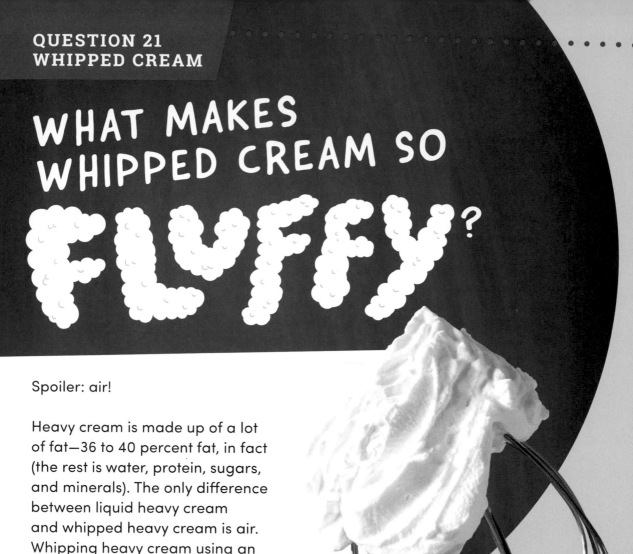

Spoiler: air!

Heavy cream is made up of a lot of fat—36 to 40 percent fat, in fact (the rest is water, protein, sugars, and minerals). The only difference between liquid heavy cream and whipped heavy cream is air. Whipping heavy cream using an electric mixer or by hand creates lots and lots of tiny air bubbles. The fat in the cream holds the air bubbles in place. As more and more air bubbles form, the heavy cream expands and becomes light and fluffy.

Are there ways to make sure that your whipped cream is REALLY fluffy? Test out one cool tip in our science experiment on page 199. And then use fluffy whipped cream in a "foolish" dessert on page 202 or dollop it on top of your Peach Shortcakes on page 204.

CREAM OF THE CROP

TOTAL TIME: 30 minutes

LEVEL: ▬ ▬ ▬
▲

MATERIALS

Masking tape

Marker

2 clear drinking glasses of the same size

2 medium bowls

½ cup plus ½ cup heavy cream, chilled, measured separately

1½ teaspoons plus 1½ teaspoons sugar, measured separately

½ teaspoon plus ½ teaspoon vanilla extract, measured separately

Electric mixer

Rubber spatula

Liquid measuring cup

Instant-read thermometer (optional)

Discover the secret to making the lightest, fluffiest whipped cream in this airy experiment. You can substitute whipping cream for the heavy cream, but do NOT substitute light cream or half-and-half—the experiment won't work. If you don't have an electric mixer, you can use a whisk to whip the cream by hand—be prepared for a workout! It will take a few minutes longer.

LET'S GO!

1 MAKE A PREDICTION Which do you think will make fluffier whipped cream, cold heavy cream or room-temperature heavy cream? Why do you think so?

2 Use masking tape and marker to label 1 glass "Room Temperature" and the other "Cold."

3 In medium bowl, combine ½ cup heavy cream, 1½ teaspoons sugar, and ½ teaspoon vanilla. Use electric mixer on medium-low speed to whip cream for about 1 minute. Increase speed to high and whip until cream is smooth and thick, about 1 minute. Stop mixer and lift beaters out of cream. If whipped cream clings to beaters and makes soft peaks that stand up on their own (see photo, page 200), you're done. If not, keep beating and check again in 30 seconds.

4 Use rubber spatula to gently scoop whipped cream into glass labeled "Cold." Clean rubber spatula and beaters.

KEEP GOING! ↷

SOFT PEAKS

Whipped cream is done when you see soft peaks on the ends of the beaters that stand up on their own but have a curve or droop at the top.

Eat Your Experiment!

Spoon one or both batches of whipped cream on **fresh berries**, an **ice cream sundae**, our **Peach Shortcakes** (page 204), or your favorite dessert.

5 Add remaining ½ cup heavy cream to liquid measuring cup. Heat cream in microwave at 50 percent power until cream feels neutral to touch (not warm and not cold), about 20 seconds. (Cream should register about 70 degrees—room temperature—on instant-read thermometer.)

6 Combine room-temperature cream, remaining 1½ teaspoons sugar, and remaining ½ teaspoon vanilla in medium bowl. Whip cream, following directions in step 3. (It's possible that the room-temperature heavy cream will not reach soft peaks, especially if you are using pasteurized heavy cream instead of ultra-pasteurized heavy cream. If you've whipped the cream for 2½ minutes and it still has not reached soft peaks, stop and proceed with step 7.)

7 Use rubber spatula to gently scoop whipped cream into glass labeled "Room Temperature."

8 **OBSERVE YOUR RESULTS** Compare your 2 batches of whipped cream: Which has more volume (fills up more of the glass), the whipped cream made from cold heavy cream or the whipped cream made from room-temperature heavy cream? Which batch looks lighter and fluffier?

UNDERSTANDING YOUR RESULTS

STOP

(Don't read until you've completed the experiment!)

THE BIG IDEAS

- Whipping heavy cream creates lots and lots of tiny air bubbles, which makes the cream expand and become light and fluffy.
- The fat in the heavy cream is firm when it's cold and soft at room temperature.
- Because fat in the heavy cream is firmer and more solid when it's cold, it can support more trapped air bubbles—and make fluffier whipped cream.

When we tried this experiment in the Recipe Lab, the whipped cream made from cold heavy cream was light and fluffy and had nearly twice the volume of the whipped cream made from room-temperature cream. Did your experiment turn out the same way?

As we learned on page 198, the only difference between liquid heavy cream and whipped heavy cream is air (the sugar and vanilla just add flavor). Whipping heavy cream adds air bubbles, which the heavy cream's fat holds in place. And more bubbles equal fluffier whipped cream.

Here's where temperature comes in: As the fat in heavy cream warms up, say from refrigerator temperature (about 40 degrees) to room temperature (about 70 degrees), it gets softer. Think about gently squeezing a stick of butter straight from the fridge versus one you've left on the counter for a couple hours. The room-temperature butter is softer and easier to squeeze, while the cold butter is firmer and holds its shape.

The warmer, softer fat in the room-temperature heavy cream can't support the air bubbles very well, so they start to collapse—the room-temperature whipped cream won't have much volume. The fat in the cold heavy cream is firmer and more solid, so it can support more trapped air bubbles—this makes for fluffier whipped cream with more volume.

recipe

STRAWBERRY FOOLS

SERVES: 4

TOTAL TIME: 1¼ hours

LEVEL: ▲

Don't be fooled—to make this classic, creamy British dessert, you'll need to carefully combine fruit and whipped cream into a sweet, fluffy treat. You can use 1¾ pounds (28 ounces) of thawed frozen sliced strawberries instead of the fresh strawberries and begin the recipe at step 2, if desired.

PREPARE INGREDIENTS

2 pounds strawberries

2 tablespoons plus 2 tablespoons sugar, measured separately

1 tablespoon lemon juice, squeezed from ½ lemon (see page 15)

1 recipe Whipped Cream (page 207)

GATHER COOKING EQUIPMENT

Cutting board

Chef's knife

2 bowls (1 large, 1 medium)

Rubber spatula

Plastic wrap

10-inch skillet

Whisk

Slotted spoon

Spoon

4 (8- to 12-ounce) glass tumblers or jars

START COOKING!

1. Place strawberries on their sides on cutting board and carefully cut off leafy green parts. Stand strawberries on cut side and slice strawberries. (If strawberries are large, cut slices in half.)

2. Place half of strawberries in medium bowl. Add 2 tablespoons sugar and use rubber spatula to stir until combined. Cover bowl with plastic wrap and place in refrigerator until ready to use.

3. Transfer remaining strawberries to 10-inch skillet. Add lemon juice and remaining 2 tablespoons sugar and use rubber spatula to stir until combined.

4. Cook over medium heat, stirring occasionally with rubber spatula, until strawberries are broken down and spatula leaves clear trail through jam mixture, 10 to 15 minutes. Turn off heat and slide skillet to cool burner.

5. Let jam cool in skillet for 5 minutes. Use rubber spatula to scrape jam into large bowl (ask an adult for help). Cover bowl with plastic wrap and place in refrigerator until chilled, at least 30 minutes or up to 24 hours.

6. When ready to make fools, make Whipped Cream (page 207). Fold whipped cream into chilled jam following photos, right.

7. Use slotted spoon to divide half of sliced strawberries evenly among glasses. Use spoon to divide all of strawberry-cream mixture evenly among glasses. Use slotted spoon to top each glass with remaining sliced strawberries. Serve.

HOW TO FOLD

1 Add about one-third of whipped cream to bowl with jam. Whisk until just combined. Add remaining whipped cream to bowl. Use rubber spatula to cut down through center of mixture to bottom of bowl.

2 Pull spatula toward you, scraping bottom and side of bowl and gently folding mixture up and over and into middle. Rotate bowl a quarter turn and repeat scraping and gently folding over. Repeat rotating and folding until components are just combined.

Fold for the Fluffiest Fools

Folding is a technique used to gently mix delicate, airy ingredients, such as whipped cream, with denser, thicker ingredients, such as the strawberry jam in this recipe. It combines the ingredients but keeps all the air right where it belongs—in your dessert!

recipe

PEACH SHORTCAKES

Fluffy biscuits piled high with sweet, juicy peaches and airy whipped cream—maybe these desserts should be called "tallcakes"?!

MAKES: 4 shortcakes

TOTAL TIME: 1½ hours

LEVEL:

PREPARE INGREDIENTS

1 pound sliced frozen peaches, thawed

¼ teaspoon ground ginger

3 tablespoons plus 1 tablespoon sugar, measured separately, plus extra for sprinkling

1½ cups (7½ ounces) all-purpose flour

1½ teaspoons baking powder

¼ teaspoon baking soda

⅛ teaspoon salt

¾ cup buttermilk

6 tablespoons unsalted butter, melted (see page 13)

Vegetable oil spray

1 recipe Whipped Cream (page 207)

GATHER COOKING EQUIPMENT

Dry measuring cups

Cutting board

Chef's knife

2 bowls (1 large microwave-safe, 1 medium)

Rubber spatula

Oven mitts

Potato masher

Rimmed baking sheet

Parchment paper

Whisk

Liquid measuring cup

Fork

Butter knife

Cooling rack

4 serving plates

Slotted spoon

START COOKING!

1. Use dry measuring cups to measure out ¾ cup peaches and transfer to cutting board. Set aside remaining peaches. Use chef's knife to roughly chop ¾ cup peaches.

2. In large microwave-safe bowl, combine chopped peaches, ground ginger, and 3 tablespoons sugar. Use rubber spatula to stir until well combined. Heat in microwave until peaches are bubbling, about 1½ minutes.

3. Use oven mitts to remove bowl from microwave. Use potato masher to crush chopped peaches (careful—bowl will be hot). Add remaining sliced peaches to bowl and use rubber spatula to stir until combined. Let sit until peaches are juicy, at least 30 minutes or up to 2 hours.

4. Meanwhile, adjust oven rack to middle position and heat oven to 450 degrees. Line rimmed baking sheet with parchment paper.

5. In medium bowl, whisk together flour, baking powder, baking soda, salt, and remaining 1 tablespoon sugar.

KEEP GOING! ↰

SPLITTING OPEN BISCUITS

You can split open biscuits just like English muffins. Because the biscuits are delicate, using a fork is easier than using a knife.

Turn biscuit on its side, then poke tip of fork gently around edge of biscuit to split open.

6. In liquid measuring cup, use fork to stir buttermilk and melted butter until butter forms small clumps.

7. Add buttermilk mixture to bowl with flour mixture. Use clean rubber spatula to stir until combined.

8. Spray inside of ½-cup dry measuring cup with vegetable oil spray. Use greased measuring cup to scoop batter and use butter knife to scrape off extra batter. Drop 4 scoops onto parchment-lined baking sheet, leaving space between biscuits. Sprinkle each biscuit generously with extra sugar.

9. Place baking sheet in oven. Bake biscuits until tops are golden brown, 14 to 16 minutes.

10. Use oven mitts to remove baking sheet from oven and place on cooling rack (ask an adult for help). Let biscuits cool on baking sheet for 10 minutes. (This is a good time to make your Whipped Cream, see page 207.)

11. When biscuits are ready, split biscuits open with clean fork following photo, above. Transfer biscuits to individual serving plates. Use slotted spoon to divide peaches evenly among biscuit bottoms. Top each with spoonful of whipped cream and 1 biscuit top. Serve.

"It was one of the most delicious things I've ever tasted in my life. The peaches were very soft and the biscuits had a nice texture." —TRIXIE, 10

WHIPPED CREAM

For great whipped cream, heavy or whipping cream is a must. And make sure that the cream is cold (see page 201). Use an electric mixer for the fastest results, although you can use a whisk and whip cream by hand—just be prepared for a workout! If using a mixer, keep the beaters low in the bowl to minimize splatters. This recipe makes about 2 cups.

TO MAKE WHIPPED CREAM In large bowl, combine 1 cup chilled **heavy cream**, 1 tablespoon **sugar**, and 1 teaspoon **vanilla extract**. Use electric mixer on medium-low speed to whip cream for 1 minute. Increase speed to high and whip until cream is smooth and thick, about 1 minute. Stop mixer and lift beaters out of cream. If cream clings to beaters and makes soft peaks that stand up on their own, you're done. If not, keep beating and check again in 30 seconds. Don't overwhip cream.

Whip It Good

The Whipped Cream recipe above warns you not to overwhip the cream. But what happens if you take whipped cream too far? (We know you're curious!) Cream, like butter and vinaigrette (see page 123), is an emulsion. It's made of tiny droplets of fat suspended in water. As you whip cream, tiny air bubbles become held in place by those droplets of fat, making it light and fluffy. But if you whip cream for too long, the emulsion of fat and water breaks! The droplets of fat clump together and separate from the liquid. The good news is that you're on your way toward making butter. The bad news is that you'll need to start your whipped cream over again, so be sure to keep a careful eye on your cream as you beat it.

DO ALL FROZEN FOODS FEEL EQUALLY Cold?

Ice cream, ice pops, sorbet—the freezer aisle is lined with lots of icy treats. They're sweet and refreshing and sometimes give us brain freeze (ouch!).

First things first: Things feel cold to us when heat is removed from our bodies. Heat always moves from warmer things to colder things. So if you're holding an ice cube, the heat will move from your hand to the ice cube. The ice cube will warm up. And the movement of heat energy out of your body is what makes your hand feel cold.

So do all frozen foods feel equally cold? Find out for yourself in the "chilly" science experiment on page 209. And then do some further freezer research with our Milk Chocolate Fudge Pops (page 212) and Mango-Lime Sorbet (page 214).

CHILL OUT

Do all frozen things feel equally cold? Melt your mind with this surprising sensory experiment. If you'd like to do this experiment with multiple people, you'll need one set of materials for each person.

TOTAL TIME: 5 minutes, plus 4 hours freezing time before you begin

LEVEL:

MATERIALS

- 1 ice cube
- 2 zipper-lock plastic bags
- 1 (2-tablespoon) cube of butter
- Instant-read thermometer

LET'S GO!

1 Place ice cube in 1 zipper-lock plastic bag. Place cube of butter in second zipper-lock plastic bag. Seal each bag, removing as much air as possible. Place bags in freezer. Freeze for at least 4 hours.

2 MAKE A PREDICTION Do you think the frozen butter will feel colder, warmer, or the same as the ice cube when you hold them both in your hands? Why do you think so?

KEEP GOING! ↷

MEASURING TEMPERATURE

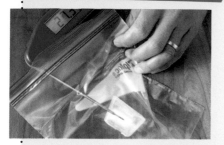

To measure the temperature of the ice cube or frozen butter, open the zipper-lock bag and place the tip of the thermometer against the surface of the ice cube or butter. Are they the same temperature or different temperatures? When you're done, reseal the zipper-lock bags.

3 OBSERVE YOUR RESULTS Remove zipper-lock bags from freezer. Open bags and use instant-read thermometer to measure temperature of ice cube and butter (see photo, left). Reseal zipper-lock bags, removing as much air as possible.

4 Close your eyes. Keeping ice cube and butter in their bags, ask grown-up to place ice cube in 1 of your hands and butter in your other hand. Hold them for 15 seconds.

5 What do you notice? Does 1 hand feel colder than the other or do they feel the same? Open your hands. Are you surprised by which hand is holding the butter and which hand is holding the ice cube? How do your results compare with your prediction?

STOP UNDERSTANDING YOUR RESULTS
(Don't read until you've completed the experiment!)

THE BIG IDEAS

- Heat moves from warmer things to colder things. The movement of heat energy out of your body is what makes you feel cold.
- It takes a lot more energy to heat ice (frozen water) than to heat the same amount of frozen butter.
- More energy moves from your warm hand to the ice cube than from your warm hand to the frozen butter—that's why the ice cube feels colder than the frozen butter, even though they're both the same temperature.

 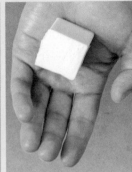

Whoa—that was weird, right? When we tried this experiment in the Recipe Lab, everyone agreed that the ice cube felt WAY colder than the frozen butter. The butter and the ice cube were in the same freezer, and when we measured their temperatures, they were both 27 degrees. How can the ice cube possibly feel colder than the frozen butter?

As we learned on page 208, things feel cold when heat is removed from our bodies. So the ice cube (frozen water) feels colder in your hand than the frozen butter because water needs a LOT of heat energy to warm up—way more heat energy than fat needs to warm up. And so butter, which is made of about 80 percent fat and only about 15 percent water, needs a much smaller amount of energy to warm up. Here's one way to think about it: Say you and a friend each have a bucket you want to fill up with water. Your bucket is a lot bigger than your friend's bucket, so you need a lot more water (and time!) to fill it to the top. Your bucket is like the ice cube! Your friend's bucket is like butter. You each pour water (heat energy) into your buckets, but you

need to pour more than your friend. To warm up ice even a little bit, you need to fill up a big bucket with heat energy. To get the same amount of butter to the same temperature, you need to fill up only a small bucket with heat energy.

In our experiment, that heat energy comes from your nice warm hands. A lot of heat energy has to move from your hand to the ice to warm it up—that makes your hand feel very cold. Warming the frozen butter takes a lot less heat energy, so a smaller amount of heat energy moves from your hand to the frozen butter, and your hand doesn't feel quite as cold.

When you're eating frozen foods, how cold they feel in your mouth depends on how much water versus fat they contain. For example, our Milk Chocolate Fudge Pops (page 212) contain milk, cocoa powder, and chocolate chips—three ingredients that contain fat, so they taste chilly and creamy but not as cold as our Mango-Lime Sorbet (page 214), which doesn't contain any fat but does contain lots of water!

recipe

MILK CHOCOLATE FUDGE POPS

These frozen treats are cool to make but don't feel supercold when you eat them! Two types of chocolate create a fudge pop with a smooth texture and lots of chocolate flavor.

MAKES: Six 3-ounce ice pops

TOTAL TIME: 35 minutes, plus 8 hours freezing time

LEVEL:

PREPARE INGREDIENTS

- ½ cup (3½ ounces) sugar
- 3 tablespoons unsweetened cocoa powder
- 4 teaspoons cornstarch
  Pinch salt
- 2 cups whole milk
- ¼ cup (1½ ounces) milk chocolate chips
- ½ teaspoon vanilla extract

GATHER COOKING EQUIPMENT

- Medium saucepan
- Whisk
- Rubber spatula
- 4-cup liquid measuring cup
- 6 ice pop molds, about 3 ounces each
- 6 ice pop sticks

Divide mixture evenly among six 3-ounce ice pop molds. Insert 1 stick into center of each mold. Cover molds and freeze until firm, at least 8 hours.

START COOKING!

1. In medium saucepan, whisk together sugar, cocoa powder, cornstarch, and salt. Add milk and chocolate chips to saucepan.

2. Bring chocolate mixture to simmer over medium heat, whisking occasionally (small bubbles should break often across surface of mixture). Cook until mixture is thickened, about 2 minutes.

3. Turn off heat and slide saucepan to cool burner. Carefully whisk in vanilla.

4. Let mixture cool for 10 minutes. Use rubber spatula to scrape chocolate mixture into liquid measuring cup (ask an adult for help).

5. Fill and cover ice pop molds following photo, above. Place in freezer and freeze until firm, at least 8 hours or up to 5 days.

6. When ready to serve, hold each mold under warm running water for 30 seconds to thaw. Slide fudge pop out of mold and serve.

"Cold" That Thought!

These chocolaty fudge pops are definitely cold, but you might have noticed that they don't feel as cold in your mouth as, say, an ice cube or a spoonful of Mango-Lime Sorbet (page 214). Frozen foods that contain more fat feel less cold than frozen foods with less fat, even if they're the same temperature (see page 211). Three ingredients in these fudge pops—cocoa powder, whole milk, and chocolate chips—all contain some fat. (Check out the nutritional label on each ingredient's package—can you find where it lists how much fat is in a serving of each ingredient?) This small amount of fat not only makes these fudge pops feel less cold as you eat them but also gives them their creamy texture.

recipe

MANGO–LIME SORBET

This sweet, scoopable, dairy-free frozen treat gets its smooth texture from some sugary science.

MAKES: 1 quart

TOTAL TIME: 45 minutes, plus 14 hours freezing time

LEVEL:

PREPARE INGREDIENTS

- ¾ cup water
- ¼ cup lime juice, squeezed from 2 limes (see page 15)
- 5 cups (25 ounces) frozen mango chunks, thawed
- 1¼ cups (8¾ ounces) sugar
- ⅛ teaspoon salt

GATHER COOKING EQUIPMENT

- 4-cup liquid measuring cup
- Fine-mesh strainer
- Large bowl
- Food processor
- Ladle
- 2 ice cube trays
- Butter knife
- Rubber spatula
- Quart-size storage container

START COOKING!

1. Combine water and lime juice in 4-cup liquid measuring cup. Set fine-mesh strainer over large bowl.

2. Add half of thawed mango chunks, half of sugar, and half of salt to food processor. Lock lid into place. Hold down pulse button for 1 second, then release. Repeat until mango chunks are broken down, about five 1-second pulses.

3. Turn on processor. With processor running, pour half of water mixture through feed tube and continue to process until sugar has dissolved and mixture is smooth, about 1 minute. Stop processor. Remove lid and carefully remove processor blade (ask an adult for help).

4. Strain mango mixture through fine-mesh strainer set over bowl following photo, right.

5. Repeat steps 2 through 4 with remaining mango chunks, sugar, salt, and water mixture.

6. Transfer strained mango mixture to now-empty liquid measuring cup. Pour mango mixture into 2 ice cube trays. Place in freezer and freeze until solid, at least 8 hours or overnight.

7. Remove ice cube trays from freezer and let sit on counter until softened slightly, 15 to 20 minutes.

8. Use butter knife to loosen cubes from ice cube trays and transfer cubes to clean processor. Lock lid into place. Hold down pulse button for 1 second, then release. Repeat until cubes begin to break down, about ten 1-second pulses.

9. Turn on processor and process until cubes are mostly broken down, about 30 seconds. Stop processor. Remove lid and use rubber spatula to scrape down sides of processor bowl and break up any cubes that are stuck together. Lock lid back into place and process until smooth, about 1 minute. Stop processor.

10. Remove lid and carefully remove processor blade (ask an adult for help). Use rubber spatula to scrape sorbet into quart-size storage container. Place in freezer and freeze until firm, at least 6 hours or overnight. Serve. (Sorbet can be frozen in airtight container for up to 1 week.)

STRAINING SORBET

Pour processed mango mixture into fine-mesh strainer set over large bowl. Use ladle to stir and press mixture to push liquid through strainer into bowl. Discard solids in strainer.

Nice Ice

Sorbet ("sore-BAY") is a frozen dessert made from fruit and sugar. It doesn't contain any fat, but it does contain a lot of water. This is why it tastes REALLY cold in your mouth! But if its ingredients are full of water, why isn't the frozen sorbet hard and solid like an ice cube? The scientific secret to sorbet's silky texture is . . . sugar. Sugar not only makes sorbet sweet but also makes it smooth and scoopable instead of hard and icy. The sugar dissolves in the liquid released from the chopped-up fruit. As the sorbet mixture freezes, the dissolved sugar does two things: It makes sure the ice crystals that form are tiny, and it lowers the freezing point of water to below 32 degrees, which means that some water will always stay liquid. All this science gives you smoother, more scoopable sorbet.

HOW DOES Gelatin WORK?

Gelatin is an unsung culinary hero—you'll find it in desserts from pudding to panna cotta to, of course, Jell-O. You don't taste it or smell it, but without gelatin, none of these foods would have its signature solid, slightly jiggly texture.

What is it? Gelatin is a kind of protein. It's made up of long, thin molecules (see page 11). When it's cold, it's a solid. When it's hot, it's a liquid. Find out exactly how gelatin can impact the texture of food in our science experiment on page 217.

And then step into the magical world of gelatin's possibilities by making a Mirror Cake (page 220) with a glaze that is as reflective as a mirror and looks just like a galaxy. Also try our Edible Spheres (page 228), which use gelatin to turn any of your favorite liquids (juice, chocolate syrup, coconut milk) into perfectly spherical little balls to sprinkle on top of ice cream, yogurt, or other desserts.

CAN'T WE ALL JUST "GEL" ALONG?

TOTAL TIME: 30 minutes, plus 1 hour chilling time

LEVEL:

MATERIALS

- Large glass
- Ice
- Water
- Masking tape
- Marker
- 3 small microwave-safe bowls
- 1-teaspoon measuring spoon
- 3 teaspoons unflavored gelatin
- Liquid measuring cup
- Spoon
- Oven mitts
- Fine-mesh strainer

In this experiment, discover how gelatin, a tiny molecule, can have a huge impact on food's texture.

LET'S GO!

1 Fill large glass with ice and water. Set aside.

2 **MAKE A PREDICTION** What do you think will happen when you combine gelatin with hot water, room-temperature water, and ice water?

3 Use masking tape and marker to label 1 small bowl "Room Temperature," second small bowl "Hot," and third small bowl "Cold." Add 1 teaspoon gelatin to each bowl.

4 Add ¼ cup (2 ounces) room-temperature water to bowl labeled "Room Temperature." Use spoon to stir gelatin and water until well combined.

KEEP GOING! ↷

QUESTION 23
GELATIN

HOW TO MEASURE ICE WATER

Hold fine-mesh strainer above liquid measuring cup. Pour ice water through strainer until you have ¼ cup (2 ounces) ice water. Discard ice and remaining water.

5 Add ¼ cup (2 ounces) room-temperature water to bowl labeled "Hot." Use clean spoon to stir gelatin and water until combined. Heat gelatin mixture in microwave until steaming, 30 to 60 seconds. Use oven mitts to remove bowl from microwave and let cool slightly. Use spoon to stir mixture until well combined.

---

6 Measure ¼ cup (2 ounces) ice water following photo, left. Discard ice and remaining water. Add ice water to bowl labeled "Cold." Use clean spoon to stir gelatin and ice water until well combined.

---

7 **OBSERVE YOUR RESULTS** Look closely at 3 gelatin mixtures and use spoon to stir each mixture. What do you notice? How do the mixtures look similar or different?

---

8 Place bowls in refrigerator and chill for at least 1 hour.

---

9 Remove bowls from refrigerator and observe your 3 gelatin mixtures again. Use spoon to stir and scoop each mixture, making sure to scrape along bottom of each bowl. How have the mixtures changed during their time in the refrigerator? Do any of the bowls look like a dessert you've seen before? Which one(s)?

STOP UNDERSTANDING YOUR RESULTS
(Don't read until you've completed the experiment!)

THE BIG IDEAS

- When gelatin is warm, it's a liquid. When it's cold, it's a solid.
- Mixing gelatin with a hot liquid lets it fully dissolve so that, when it cools, it forms a smooth, clear, solid gel.
- As dissolved gelatin cools, its protein molecules get tangled, forming a "mesh" that traps tiny bits of liquid inside so that the liquid can't move or flow.

Room-Temperature Water

Hot Water

Cold Water

When we conducted this experiment in the Recipe Lab, the gelatin mixed with hot water set into a smooth, shiny, clear solid. The gelatin mixed with room-temperature water had an opaque, solid layer on the bottom of the bowl and liquid on the top of the bowl. And the gelatin mixed with ice water never fully solidified—it stayed a chunky liquid.

Gelatin is a kind of protein that's made up of long, thin molecules. But what gives gelatin its ability to turn liquids into smooth, clear solids, such as Jell-O? First, gelatin is a water magnet—it absorbs water really easily. Second, when gelatin is warm, it's a liquid, and when it's cold, it's a solid called a "gel" (get it?).

When you mix gelatin with a cool liquid, the liquid makes its way into each teeny-tiny granule of gelatin, hydrating it. (This is called "blooming" the gelatin.) At this point, the gelatin mixture looks opaque, meaning that you can't see through it. Just adding water isn't enough to make the gelatin dissolve in the liquid. You need to add heat, too.

Heating the mixture dissolves the gelatin in the water, forming a smooth, transparent, pourable liquid. When gelatin is mixed with a hot liquid, its molecules move around a lot—the liquid stays liquid. As the temperature gets colder, the gelatin molecules slow down and start to get tangled, kind of like the cord of your headphones when they're in your pocket. Eventually, the gelatin molecules get so tangled that they trap the liquid inside. The liquid can't move around or flow: It becomes a solid.

recipe

MIRROR CAKE

Mirror, mirror on the wall, who is the shiniest cake of all? Thanks to gelatin, it's this one! To get the boldest colors, make sure to use gel food coloring. We love using our Chocolate Layer Cake (page 224) and Vanilla Frosting (page 227) here, but you can use boxed cake mix and store-bought frosting instead. Be sure to follow How to Frost a Layer Cake (page 226) to make a smooth base for the mirror glaze.

SERVES: 16 to 20

TOTAL TIME: 45 minutes, plus time to make layer cake, plus chilling time

LEVEL:

PREPARE INGREDIENTS

1 9-inch frosted layer cake (see Chocolate Layer Cake, page 224)

2 tablespoons unflavored gelatin

¼ cup (2 ounces) plus ½ cup (4 ounces) water, measured separately

1 cup (7 ounces) sugar

½ cup sweetened condensed milk

1 tablespoon vanilla extract

1⅓ cups (8 ounces) white chocolate chips

¼ teaspoon black gel food coloring

⅛ teaspoon purple gel food coloring

⅛ teaspoon turquoise gel food coloring

GATHER COOKING EQUIPMENT

Rimmed baking sheet

Parchment paper

Cooling rack

9-inch cardboard round (see photos, page 225) or 9-inch flat plate

2 bowls (1 medium, 1 small)

Spoon

Small saucepan

Rubber spatula

Fine-mesh strainer

2 liquid measuring cups (or 2 small bowls)

Spatula

Serving platter

Chef's knife

Dish towel

START COOKING!

1. Line rimmed baking sheet with parchment paper and place cooling rack inside baking sheet. Place frosted cake on 9-inch cardboard round and place in freezer while making glaze.

2. In small bowl, use spoon to stir together gelatin and ¼ cup water. Let sit for 5 minutes.

3. Meanwhile, in small saucepan, combine sugar, sweetened condensed milk, vanilla, and remaining ½ cup water. Cook sugar mixture over medium heat, stirring occasionally with rubber spatula, until mixture starts to bubble around edges, 5 to 8 minutes. Turn off heat and slide saucepan to cool burner.

4. Use rubber spatula to scrape gelatin mixture into sugar mixture. Stir until gelatin is dissolved. Add white chocolate chips and stir until melted and mixture is smooth, about 1 minute.

5. Place fine-mesh strainer in medium bowl. Pour chocolate mixture through strainer (ask an adult for help—saucepan will be heavy); discard solids. Let glaze cool for 15 minutes, stirring occasionally to prevent skin from forming.

KEEP GOING! ↰

HOW TO MIX GLAZE

1 Add black food coloring to one liquid measuring cup and stir to combine. Clean spatula. Add purple food coloring to second liquid measuring cup and stir to combine. Clean spatula. Add turquoise food coloring to remaining glaze in bowl and stir to combine.

2 Pour black glaze into center of turquoise glaze in bowl (do not stir together). Pour purple glaze right next to black glaze in bowl (do not stir together).

6. Pour ½ cup glaze into each liquid measuring cup. Add gel food coloring to each glaze and combine in bowl following photos, left.

7. Remove cake from freezer and place on cooling rack set inside parchment-lined baking sheet. Working quickly, pour glaze over top of chilled cake (in center of cake), letting glaze drip down and coat sides of cake. Some glaze will drip onto baking sheet—that's OK!

8. Let cake sit for 5 minutes, allowing extra glaze to drip off cake. Slide spatula under cardboard round and carefully lift glazed cake. Transfer glazed cake to serving platter and place in refrigerator to chill until glaze is set and no longer sticky, about 20 minutes.

9. Remove cake from refrigerator and let sit at room temperature for at least 30 minutes or up to 24 hours before serving. To serve, run chef's knife under hot water, then wipe knife dry with dish towel (ask an adult for help). Slice cake, wetting and drying knife in between slices. Serve.

Putting the "Mirror" in Mirror Cake

The shiny, reflective surface of a mirror cake is all thanks to the magic of gelatin. When the gelatin in the Mirror Cake glaze is above 50 degrees, it's a pourable liquid. But when gelatin's temperature drops below 50 degrees, it begins to turn solid. And the colder gelatin gets, the faster it solidifies—that's why we freeze the frosted cake before pouring the glaze on top. When the warm glaze hits the cold cake, its temperature drops and the gelatin starts to become a solid. As it cools, it traps the water inside a tangled mesh of gelatin molecules. After the glaze sets in the refrigerator for 20 minutes and its temperature reaches below 50 degrees, the water trapped inside this solid gel acts like a smooth, reflective pond, puddle, or mirror!

THE BIG POUR

Working quickly, pour glaze over top of chilled cake (in center of cake) letting glaze drip down and coat sides of cake.

recipe

CHOCOLATE LAYER CAKE

We highly recommend using Dutch-processed cocoa powder in this recipe. If you use natural cocoa powder, the cake will be drier in texture and lighter in color.

SERVES: 16 to 20

TOTAL TIME: 1 hour, plus 1 hour cooling time

LEVEL:

PREPARE INGREDIENTS

Vegetable oil spray

1½ cups (7½ ounces) all-purpose flour

1½ cups (10½ ounces) sugar

1 cup (3 ounces) Dutch-processed cocoa powder

1 teaspoon baking powder

½ teaspoon baking soda

½ teaspoon salt

1½ cups (12 ounces) milk

¾ cup vegetable oil

2 large eggs

2 teaspoons vanilla extract

5 cups Vanilla Frosting (see page 227) or your favorite store-bought frosting

GATHER COOKING EQUIPMENT

Two 9-inch round metal cake pans

Two 9-inch round pieces of parchment paper (see photos, page 225)

2 bowls (1 large, 1 medium)

Whisk

Rubber spatula

Toothpick

Oven mitts

Cooling rack

Butter knife

Chef's knife

Icing spatula

START COOKING!

1. Adjust oven rack to middle position and heat oven to 325 degrees. Spray inside bottom and sides of each 9-inch round metal cake pan with vegetable oil spray. Line each cake pan with 9-inch round piece of parchment paper.

2. In medium bowl, whisk together flour, sugar, cocoa, baking powder, baking soda, and salt.

3. In large bowl, whisk together milk, oil, eggs, and vanilla.

4. Add flour mixture to milk mixture and use rubber spatula to stir until just combined and no dry flour is visible. Do not overmix.

5. Use rubber spatula to divide batter evenly between parchment-lined cake pans and smooth tops. (Spread batter out to edges of each pan to create even layer.)

6. Place cake pans in oven. Bake until toothpick inserted in center of each cake comes out clean, 34 to 36 minutes.

7. Use oven mitts to remove cake pans from oven and place on cooling rack (ask an adult for help). Let cakes cool completely in pans, about 1 hour. (This is a good time to make the Vanilla Frosting, page 227.)

8. Run butter knife around edge of each cake to loosen cake from pan. Remove cakes from their pans and discard parchment. Assemble and frost cake following photos, page 226. Cut cake into wedges and serve. (If making Mirror Cake (see page 220), follow recipe before cutting and serving cake!)

HOW TO MAKE PARCHMENT AND CARDBOARD ROUNDS

Lining cake pans with parchment paper prevents cakes from sticking and makes them easier to remove. Cardboard rounds help with moving frosted cakes from one place to another, as with our Mirror Cake (see page 220).

1 Place cake pan on sheet of parchment paper or piece of cardboard. Use pencil to trace around bottom of pan.

2 Cut out parchment or cardboard with scissors, following traced line.

An icing spatula (or offset spatula), a large spatula with a bend in the blade, is best here, but a butter knife will also work.

1 Place 1 cake layer on cardboard round or serving platter. Use icing spatula to spread 1 cup frosting over top of cake. Top with second cake layer and press gently to set.

2 Use icing spatula to spread remaining 4 cups frosting over top and sides of cake. Gently smooth out bumps around sides of cake and tidy areas where frosting on top and side merge. Then run spatula over top of cake again to smooth out any remaining bumps.

What Is Dutch-Processed Cocoa Powder?

A process called Dutching, which was invented in the 19th century by a Dutch chemist and chocolatier named Coenraad van Houten, gives cocoa powder a more chocolaty flavor and a deeper brown color. Dutching also lowers cocoa powder's acidity. Dutch-processed cocoa powder, sometimes called alkalized or European-style cocoa powder, is the best choice for most baked goods, including this chocolate cake. Using a natural (unalkalized) cocoa powder creates a drier cake that is a lighter brown color.

VANILLA FROSTING

This recipe makes enough to frost one layer cake, such as our Chocolate Layer Cake (page 224). Don't use salted butter in this recipe. You need a little salt to balance the sugar but not as much as is found in salted butter.

MAKES: 5 cups

TOTAL TIME: 20 minutes

LEVEL:

PREPARE INGREDIENTS

- 1 pound (4 sticks) unsalted butter, cut into 20 pieces and softened (see page 13)
- ¼ cup (2 ounces) heavy cream
- 1 tablespoon vanilla extract
- ¼ teaspoon salt
- 4 cups (1 pound) confectioners' (powdered) sugar

GATHER COOKING EQUIPMENT

- Electric mixer (stand mixer with paddle attachment or hand-held mixer and large bowl)
- Rubber spatula

1. In bowl of stand mixer (or large bowl if using handheld mixer), combine softened butter, cream, vanilla, and salt. Lock bowl into place and attach paddle to stand mixer, if using.

2. Start mixer on medium speed and beat until smooth, about 1 minute. Stop mixer. Use rubber spatula to scrape down bowl.

3. Start mixer on low speed. Slowly add confectioners' sugar, a little bit at a time, and beat until smooth, about 4 minutes. Increase speed to medium-high and beat until frosting is light and fluffy, about 5 minutes. Stop mixer. Remove bowl from stand mixer, if using.

Making Vanilla Frosting Ahead

Vanilla Frosting can be refrigerated for up to three days. When you're ready to use it, let the frosting soften at room temperature for 1 to 2 hours. Then, rewhip the frosting using a stand mixer with the paddle attachment or a handheld mixer on medium speed until the frosting is smooth, 2 to 5 minutes. The frosting can sit at room temperature for up to 2 hours before using.

recipe

EDIBLE SPHERES

Spherification is a cool technique that transforms liquids into solid, edible spheres. Don't substitute other types of oil for the vegetable oil. You can make edible spheres out of any water-based flavorful liquid. If your flavorful liquid is thick, like chocolate syrup or coconut milk, first mix ¼ cup of the flavorful liquid with ¼ cup of water. Then, measure from that mixture. Try sprinkling edible spheres over ice cream, yogurt, or your favorite desserts or adding them to a cold, fizzy drink.

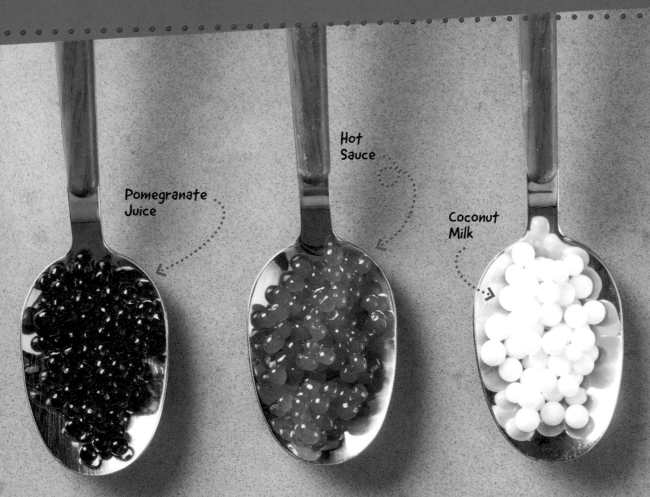

Pomegranate Juice

Hot Sauce

Coconut Milk

MAKES: About ½ cup spheres

TOTAL TIME: 45 minutes, plus 4 hours chilling time before you begin

LEVEL:

PREPARE INGREDIENTS

- 2 cups vegetable oil
- 2 tablespoons plus ¼ cup pomegranate juice, measured separately
- 1 tablespoon unflavored gelatin
- 6 cups ice

GATHER COOKING EQUIPMENT

Tall container (about 24 ounces) with lid

4 bowls (1 large, 2 medium, 1 small)

Rubber spatula

Liquid measuring cup

Oven mitts

Whisk

Funnel (optional)

Squeeze bottle

Toothpick

Fine-mesh strainer

START COOKING!

1. At least 4 hours before you want to make your spheres, pour oil into tall container, cover container, and place container in refrigerator.

2. Add 2 tablespoons pomegranate juice to small bowl. Sprinkle gelatin over surface of juice. Use rubber spatula to stir until no large lumps of gelatin remain. Set aside.

3. Add remaining ¼ cup pomegranate juice to liquid measuring cup. Heat in microwave until steaming, 30 to 45 seconds.

4. Use oven mitts to remove liquid measuring cup from microwave (ask an adult for help). Pour hot pomegranate juice into bowl with gelatin mixture. Whisk mixture until fully combined and no lumps remain.

5. Place funnel, if using, over squeeze bottle. Carefully pour gelatin mixture into squeeze bottle (ask an adult for help). Secure top on bottle. Place bottle in refrigerator for 10 to 15 minutes to let gelatin mixture thicken slightly.

KEEP GOING! ↷

MAKING SPHERES

1 Hold bottle at angle over container of oil. Gently squeeze bottle until droplets fall into oil. Each droplet should form sphere and fall to bottom. To make larger spheres, quickly drip several drops of liquid in same spot. Continue forming spheres until all liquid is used. (If gelatin mixture clogs nozzle of bottle, unscrew cap, run under warm water, and use toothpick to push out any stuck gelatin. If mixture becomes too thick, heat squeeze bottle in microwave for 5 seconds.)

2 In sink, set fine-mesh strainer over medium bowl. Carefully pour oil-sphere mixture into strainer. Use rubber spatula to scrape any remaining spheres into strainer. Discard oil.

6. Remove container of oil from refrigerator and place in center of large bowl. Arrange ice around container of oil. (Surrounding the oil with ice will keep it cold while you're forming your spheres.) Carefully remove lid from container of oil.

7. Remove squeeze bottle from refrigerator. Make and drain spheres following photos, left.

8. Fill second medium bowl about halfway with cold water. Transfer spheres from fine-mesh strainer to bowl of cold water. Use rubber spatula to gently stir spheres in water. Working over sink, gently pour water-sphere mixture back into strainer, letting water go down drain. Serve. (Leftover spheres can be stored in airtight container, covered with layer of vegetable oil, for up to 1 week. Follow steps 7 and 8 to rinse spheres before serving.)

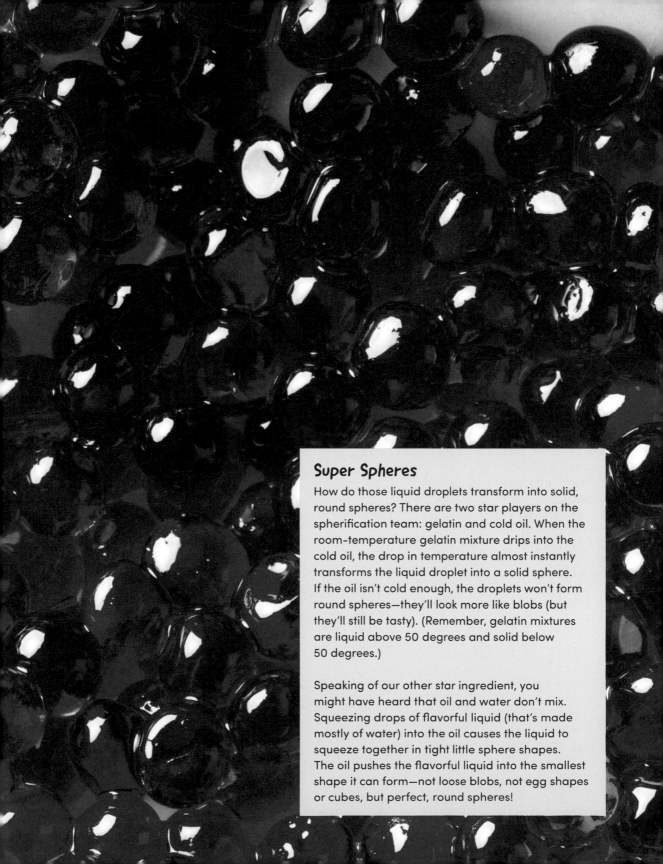

Super Spheres

How do those liquid droplets transform into solid, round spheres? There are two star players on the spherification team: gelatin and cold oil. When the room-temperature gelatin mixture drips into the cold oil, the drop in temperature almost instantly transforms the liquid droplet into a solid sphere. If the oil isn't cold enough, the droplets won't form round spheres—they'll look more like blobs (but they'll still be tasty). (Remember, gelatin mixtures are liquid above 50 degrees and solid below 50 degrees.)

Speaking of our other star ingredient, you might have heard that oil and water don't mix. Squeezing drops of flavorful liquid (that's made mostly of water) into the oil causes the liquid to squeeze together in tight little sphere shapes. The oil pushes the flavorful liquid into the smallest shape it can form—not loose blobs, not egg shapes or cubes, but perfect, round spheres!

CONVERSIONS & EQUIVALENTS

The recipes in this book were developed using standard U.S. measures. The charts below offer equivalents for U.S. and metric measures. All conversions are approximate and have been rounded up or down to the nearest whole number.

VOLUME CONVERSIONS

U.S.	METRIC
1 teaspoon	5 milliliters
2 teaspoons	10 milliliters
1 tablespoon	15 milliliters
2 tablespoons	30 milliliters
¼ cup	59 milliliters
⅓ cup	79 milliliters
½ cup	118 milliliters
¾ cup	177 milliliters
1 cup	237 milliliters
2 cups (1 pint)	473 milliliters
4 cups (1 quart)	1 liter
4 quarts (1 gallon)	4 liters

WEIGHT CONVERSIONS

U.S.	METRIC
½ ounce	14 grams
¾ ounce	21 grams
1 ounce	28 grams
2 ounces	57 grams
3 ounces	85 grams
4 ounces	113 grams
5 ounces	142 grams
6 ounces	170 grams
8 ounces	227 grams
10 ounces	283 grams
12 ounces	340 grams
16 ounces (1 pound)	454 grams

OVEN TEMPERATURES

FAHRENHEIT	CELSIUS	GAS MARK
225°	105°	¼
250°	120°	½
275°	135°	1
300°	150°	2
325°	165°	3
350°	180°	4
375°	190°	5
400°	200°	6
425°	220°	7
450°	230°	8
475°	245°	9

CONVERTING TEMPERATURES FROM AN INSTANT-READ THERMOMETER

We include doneness temperatures in some recipes in this book. We recommend an instant-read thermometer for the job. To convert a temperature from Fahrenheit to Celsius, subtract 32 from the Fahrenheit reading, then divide the result by 1.8.

Example
"Roast chicken until thighs register 175°F"
To Convert
175 − 32 = 143
143 ÷ 1.8 = 79.44°C, rounded down to 79°C

MEET OUR TEAM

Introducing America's Test Kitchen Kids!

This book was created by a group of passionate chefs, writers, editors, scientists, educators, designers, illustrators, and photographers. Our mission is to create a new generation of empowered cooks, engaged eaters, and curious experimenters.

MOLLY BIRNBAUM
Editor in Chief

I love to bake, and I love to weigh my ingredients as I bake. It's satisfying. It's accurate. It's science! (I highly recommend the Cinnamon Swirl Bread on page 26. I've made it three times since I first read the recipe!)

ALI VELEZ ALDERFER
Senior Editor

When I'm in the kitchen baking with my very curious 3-year-old, I love that there are precise measurements and steps to follow. Using well-tested science to create something delicious is extremely satisfying.

SUZANNAH MCFERRAN
Executive Food Editor

My most memorable moment for this book was doing late-night tests of the mirror glaze for the cover, in search of the perfect pour. I was at home with my daughter, Chloe, who filmed the results on my phone!

AFTON CYRUS
Senior Editor

I loved working on the recipes for Cinnamon Swirl Bread (page 26) (I love baking bread!), Chana Masala (page 100) (full of delicious spices), and Risotto with Parmesan and Herbs (page 140) (a fancy, restaurant-style dish that we made easy for kids).

KRISTIN SARGIANIS
Executive Editor

Developing our recipe for Edible Spheres (page 228) was superchallenging, but I'm thrilled with how it turned out. The spheres add fun pops of color, texture, and flavor to food—plus they're delicious examples of chemistry and physics at work!

ANDREA RIVERA WAWRZYN Test Cook

I love uncovering kitchen mysteries. Understanding what is happening in the skillet or the oven can help make a better, more flexible cook in the kitchen. I loved developing Skillet Cheeseburger Macaroni (page 74) and Cloud Eggs (page 36)!

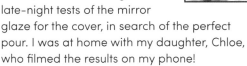

CASSANDRA LOFTLIN
Test Cook

Milk Chocolate Fudge Pops (page 212) are one of my favorite frozen desserts. This version was based on ones I enjoyed as a kid. Since developing this recipe, I make these often. They're a treat that my whole family enjoys, especially my grandmother. Without science, I would have never figured out how to make the perfect pop.

KATY O'HARA
Assistant Editor

I loved learning interesting science facts about foods I eat all the time. I wrote the sidebar "Pop Goes the Popcorn" for our Stovetop Popcorn recipe (page 158), and I was so intrigued to learn about what that popcorn "pop" sound is caused by. (Plus, it gave me a great excuse to watch lots of videos of popcorn popping in superslow motion. Hypnotizing!)

TESS BERGER
Assistant Editor

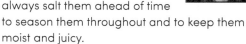

When I'm pan-frying chicken breasts or grilling a steak, I always salt them ahead of time to season them throughout and to keep them moist and juicy.

JACK BISHOP
Chief Creative Officer

My vegetable garden is a delicious science experiment. Should I start with seeds or small plants from the garden center? Water once a day or every other day? Pick the zucchini when they are the size of my pointer finger or wait until they are as big as my whole hand? Which varieties do best in a sunny spot? I test many variables and then adjust how I garden with the goal of growing tastier veggies and increasing my yield—there are never enough carrots or eggplant.

LINDSEY TIMKO CHANDLER
Design Director

I love how there is always something new to learn when it comes to science and cooking. You think you've seen it all, and then BOOM—you learn how to make an egg look like a cloud or turn hot sauce into an edible sphere!

ALLISON BOALES
Deputy Art Director

I had so much fun working on the cover for this book. Seeing how the mirror glaze produced different patterns every time was exciting and beautiful. I can't wait to make this recipe at home!

JULIE BOZZO COTE
Photography Director

I love working with kids to show the joy of science during photo shoots. Watching our friend Sammi cutting onions with goggles on (page 51) was a blast; he looked like such a cool scientist. At home, my son loves it when I tear up cutting onions because it is such proof that science is always working with us in the background.

GABI HOMONOFF
Illustrator

My favorite part of working on this book was creating all kinds of food-inspired typography!

KEVIN WHITE
Photographer

Since we photograph steps for each recipe, I was able to see firsthand how easy a lot of the recipes are. Although this is a book for young chefs, I am definitely going to make some of these recipes at home for myself.

RECIPE STATS

Per Serving		Calories	Fat (g)	Saturated Fat (g)	Sodium (mg)	Carbohydrates (g)	Fiber (g)	Total Sugar (g)	Added Sugar (g)	Protein (g)
Part 1: BREAKFAST										
Crepes	serves 4	270	13	6	240	27	0	6	1	11
Cinnamon Swirl Bread	serves 10	240	6	3.5	250	41	0	15	14	5
Huevos Rancheros	serves 4	380	22	7	1490	31	5	10	2	17
Cloud Eggs	serves 4	70	5	1.5	105	0	0	0	0	6
Smoothie Bowls	serves 2	180	1.5	1	90	43	2	27	5	3
Mixed Berry Muffins	per muffin	270	9	6	280	42	1	19	17	5
Part 2: LUNCH, DINNER & SIDES										
Caramelized Onions	per 2 tablespoons	50	2.5	0	125	7	1	3	0	1
Pickled Red Onions	per 2 tablespoons	5	0	0	150	2	0	1	1	0
Pan-Seared Strip Steaks	serves 4	240	9	3	170	0	0	0	0	39
Ham and Cheese Panini	serves 1	450	31	14	1030	22	0	1	0	22
Roasted Cauliflower	serves 4	140	11	1.5	270	10	4	4	0	4
Skillet Pizza	serves 3	600	30	9	1700	58	3	6	1	23
Skillet Cheeseburger Macaroni	serves 4	610	27	13	1760	49	3	6	0	37
Salmon with Miso-Orange Sauce	serves 4	400	23	5	600	10	0	7	3	36
Pasta with Meat Sauce	serves 6	490	16	5	1000	72	6	11	0	28
Salt-and-Vinegar Smashed Potatoes	serves 4	290	14	2	640	36	4	3	0	4
Cheesy Zucchini-Carrot Crisps	serves 4	80	3.5	2	380	8	1	2	0	5
Chicken Fajitas	serves 4	490	17	4	1530	56	2	5	0	28
Chana Masala	serves 6	210	10	1	740	24	7	2	0	8
Tiny Chicken Tenders	serves 4	390	16	3	580	27	0	1	0	32
Tacos de Tinga de Pollo (Chicken Tinga Tacos)	serves 4	430	16	2.5	1030	34	2	6	0	38
Spaghetti Aglio e Olio	serves 6	380	14	1.5	160	56	3	1	0	10
One-Pot Shells with Peas and Sausage	serves 4	580	14	4.5	1780	76	6	6	0	37

Per Serving		Calories	Fat (g)	Saturated Fat (g)	Sodium (mg)	Carbohydrates (g)	Fiber (g)	Total Sugar (g)	Added Sugar (g)	Protein (g)
Miso-Honey Vinaigrette with Salad	serves 4	140	12	1.5	135	6	1	3	1	2
Buttery Sugar Snap Peas	serves 4	100	6	3.5	150	9	3	5	0	3
Garlicky Kale	serves 4	160	12	1.5	330	11	4	3	0	5
Pan-Steamed Broccoli with Lemon	serves 4	80	6	3.5	320	6	3	2	0	3
Rainbow Grain Bowls	serves 4	620	29	3.5	550	88	14	9	4	11
Risotto with Parmesan and Herbs	serves 4	260	9	4.5	850	38	1	2	0	9
Simple White Beans with Garlic	serves 6	210	10	1.5	110	23	13	1	0	8
Black Bean Burgers	serves 4	490	24	3.5	1080	58	2	5	0	15

Part 3: SNACKS & DRINKS

Per Serving		Calories	Fat (g)	Saturated Fat (g)	Sodium (mg)	Carbohydrates (g)	Fiber (g)	Total Sugar (g)	Added Sugar (g)	Protein (g)
Stovetop Popcorn	serves 6	70	3	0	0	10	2	0	0	2
Chocolate-Covered Popcorn	serves 8	200	7	4.5	115	34	1	27	27	1
Corn Tortilla Chips	serves 4	80	1	0	150	17	0	0	0	2
Frico Chips	serves 4	40	3.5	2	105	0	0	0	0	2
Chunky Guacamole	serves 8	120	11	1.5	150	7	5	1	0	2
Fruit Salad with Vanilla and Mint	serves 4	120	0	0	0	30	4	19	4	2
Sparkling Pink Lemonade	serves 1	80	0	0	40	21	0	20	19	0
Ginger Ale	serves 1	160	0	0	65	42	0	38	38	0

Part 4: SWEETS

Per Serving		Calories	Fat (g)	Saturated Fat (g)	Sodium (mg)	Carbohydrates (g)	Fiber (g)	Total Sugar (g)	Added Sugar (g)	Protein (g)
Crispy Chocolate Chip Cookies	serves 12	130	6	3.5	110	18	1	10	10	1
Chewy Chocolate Cookies	serves 12	120	5	3	75	18	1	13	13	2
Strawberry Fools	serves 4	230	12	7	10	33	5	26	14	2
Peach Shortcakes	serves 4	520	28	18	370	60	2	27	14	8
Milk Chocolate Fudge Pops	serves 6	160	5	3	65	28	0	24	20	3
Mango-Lime Sorbet	per ½ cup	180	0	0	35	47	1	45	31	0
Mirror Cake	serves 20	590	33	16	180	69	0	61	49	5
Edible Spheres	serves 8	10	0	0	0	2	0	1	0	1
Chocolate Layer Cake	serves 20	460	29	14	160	48	0	40	39	3
Vanilla Frosting	per 2 tablespoons	130	9	6	15	12	0	12	12	0

INDEX